# Recent Research in Psychology

D1995186

Ernest McDaniel Chris Lawrence

# Levels of Cognitive Complexity

## An Approach to the Measurement of Thinking

Springer-Verlag
New York Berlin Heidelberg
London Paris Tokyo Hong Kong

Ernest McDaniel
Department of Educational Studies
Purdue University
West Lafayette, Indiana, 47907, USA

Chris Lawrence
Department of Educational Studies
Purdue University
West Lafayette, Indiana, 47907, USA

Library of Congress Cataloging in Publication Data
McDaniel, Ernest.
Levels of cognitive complexity : an approach to the measurement of thinking / Ernest McDaniel, Chris Lawrence.
p. cm. — (Recent research in psychology)
Includes bibliographical references.
1. Thought and thinking. 2. Thought and thinking—Testing. 3. Human information processing. I. Lawrence, Chris, 1950- II. Title. III. Series.
BF441.M38 1990
153.4′2′0287—dc20 90-34253
CIP

Printed on acid-free paper

© 1990 Springer-Verlag New York Inc.
All rights reserved. This work may not be translated or copied in whole or in part without the written permission of the publisher (Springer-Verlag New York, Inc., 175 Fifth Avenue, New York, NY 10010, USA), except for brief excerpts in connection with reviews or scholarly analysis. Use in connection with any form of information and retrieval, electronic adaptation, computer software, or by similar or dissimilar methodology now known or hereafter developed is forbidden.
The use of general descriptive names, trade names, trademarks, etc., in this publication, even if the former are not especially identified, is not to be taken as a sign that such names, as understood by the Trade Marks and Merchandise Marks Act, may accordingly be used freely by anyone.

Camera-ready copy provided by the authors.
Printed and bound by Edwards Brothers, Inc., Ann Arbor, Michigan.
Printed in the United States of America.

9 8 7 6 5 4 3 2 1

ISBN 0-387-97301-X Springer-Verlag New York Berlin Heidelberg
ISBN 3-540-97301-X Springer Verlag Berlin Heidelberg New York

Ernest McDaniel Chris Lawrence
Editors

# Levels of Cognitive Complexity

## An Approach to the Measurement of Thinking

Springer-Verlag
New York Berlin Heidelberg
London Paris Tokyo Hong Kong

Ernest McDaniel
Department of Educational Studies
Purdue University
West Lafayette, Indiana, 47907, USA

Chris Lawrence
Department of Educational Studies
Purdue University
West Lafayette, Indiana, 47907, USA

Library of Congress Cataloging in Publication Data
McDaniel, Ernest.
Levels of cognitive complexity : an approach to the measurement of thinking / Ernest McDaniel, Chris Lawrence.
p. cm. — (Recent research in psychology)
Includes bibliographical references.
1. Thought and thinking. 2. Thought and thinking—Testing. 3. Human information processing. I. Lawrence, Chris, 1950- II. Title. III. Series.
BF441.M38 1990
153.4'2'0287—dc20 90-34253
CIP

Printed on acid-free paper

© 1990 Springer-Verlag New York Inc.
All rights reserved. This work may not be translated or copied in whole or in part without the written permission of the publisher (Springer-Verlag New York, Inc., 175 Fifth Avenue, New York, NY 10010, USA), except for brief excerpts in connection with reviews or scholarly analysis. Use in connection with any form of information and retrieval, electronic adaptation, computer software, or by similar or dissimilar methodology now known or hereafter developed is forbidden.
The use of general descriptive names, trade names, trademarks, etc., in this publication, even if the former are not especially identified, is not to be taken as a sign that such names, as understood by the Trade Marks and Merchandise Marks Act, may accordingly be used freely by anyone.

Camera-ready copy provided by the editors.
Printed and bound by Edwards Brothers, Inc., Ann Arbor, Michigan.
Printed in the United States of America.

9 8 7 6 5 4 3 2 1

ISBN 0-387-97301-X Springer-Verlag New York Berlin Heidelberg
ISBN 3-540-97301-X Springer Verlag Berlin Heidelberg New York

*"The careful appraisal of critical thinking should be an extremely important endeavor in our society - one worthy of a great deal of careful research adequately backed by financial support. For as our world becomes increasingly complex and technical, the need for individuals with this capability will surely expand. Indeed, the development and identification of this characteristic could become the central focus of education and employee selection"*

*...... Helmstadter, 1985*

# *Acknowledgements*

We wish to express our deep appreciation to The American Honda Foundation of Torrance, California for a grant that made it possible to initiate and sustain this research. We particularly appreciate Ms. Kathryn Carey's warm, personal touch in administering the grant for the American Honda Foundation.

We want to extend thanks to The Simon Wiesenthal Center of Los Angeles for special permission to edit and use their material in this research.

Earlier members of the research team who did much of the foundation work for this study are Penny Armstrong, Yvonne Ferrerya, Ann Peregrine, Chyng-Pyng Shiang, and Tamara Thompson. Others who have collected data and shared results with us are Laura Durkin, Amy Nimlos, Kurt Taube, Charlene Walahan, and Judith Wood.

Special thanks is extended to Dick Meister, a gifted social studies teacher in the West Lafayette High School who originally suggested use of Genocide and The Bomb Factories, two videotapes which have served as important stimulus materials for the work reported here.

Bill Castor and Dick Henshaw, Roosevelt Middle School, Monticello, Indiana, have been continuing colleagues in the field, lending their interest and their eighth grade social studies classes to this project.

Jason Brewer, social studies teacher at Harrison High School, Tippecanoe County School Corporation has made us feel at home in his classroom and assisted in the data collection.

# *Overview*

This monograph describes a new approach to the measurement of thinking processes. Traditionally, thinking has been defined in terms of the logical thought processes (deduction, induction, etc) which lead to warranted conclusions. The psychological processes, on the other hand, involve the individual's perceptions, intentions and information processing strategies. Traditional logical approaches appear to be most suitable for analysis of thinking in formal, highly structured problem situations. Current tests of critical thinking reflect the "logical" approach to measuring thinking.

Other investigators have defined and researched thinking in terms of the processes used in interpreting situations. These studies suggest ways of conceptualizing thinking and provide specific markers which help define levels of thinking. The information processing approach emphasizes the way situational information is perceived, selected, organized and interpreted. Using this approach, we have developed two interpretive exercises, The Holocaust and The Bomb Factories. The results of a number of studies conducted with these exercises are presented and future work is projected.

# *Contents*

# 1

# *Approaches to Studying Reasoning*

## Conceptions of Thinking

More than 85 years ago, Charles Peirce (1903), in a speech at Harvard, criticized a fellow logician for "the fundamental mistake of confounding the logical question with the psychological question. The psychological question is what processes the mind goes through. The logical question is whether the conclusion that will be reached, by applying this or that maxim, will or will not accord with the "*fact*." Historically, philosophers analyzing reasoning have fixed their attention on procedures for getting conclusions that accord with the facts. Thus, as Bruner (1986) points out, "There was no psychology of thought, only logic and a catalogue of logical errors" (p. 107).

The distinction between the logical and the psychological approach to thinking is critical to the way thinking is conceptualized and measured. The existing tests of thinking, which will be reviewed shortly, reflect the traditional view of thinking as "right reasoning." We view thinking primarily as the selection, organization and transformation of information as the individual makes sense of situations.

The distinction between the logical and psychological approaches to thinking is related to the contrast between formal logic and what others call "everyday reasoning" (Bartlett, 1958; Perkins,

1982). Whether "right thinking" defines the process employed in most everyday situations has been a subject of controversy.

Galotti (1989) discusses the differences between these two types of reasoning. Formal reasoning consists of following a set of rules within a bounded or self-contained problem. Correct or logically sound rules and established methods of inference are followed, leading to a correct answer or unambiguous solution. In formal reasoning problems, all of the information that is to be considered is explicitly given in the problem and all of the premises are supplied. Problems are solved for their own sake.

In everyday reasoning the problems are not bounded or well-defined. There are no clearly correct answers and no established procedures for solving the problems. Premises may be implicit or not given at all. Preexisting knowledge and broad concepts are used to perceive, define, and support the point of view taken. Problems usually have potential personal relevance and are investigated as a means of achieving other goals.

Each of the two approaches brings its own challenge. Within a highly defined problem situation, the challenge is to apply the rules of reasoning leading to an answer that is in accord with the facts. Within a problem situation marked by ambiguity and multiple right answers, the challenge is to formulate and address the problem in ways that are consistent with one's values, attitudes, and conceptions of the way the world works. Although the rules of reasoning enter into a decision, the way the problem is defined and the way information is selected, organized, and interpreted play the determining roles.

## Tests of Thinking

The existing tests of critical thinking for adolescents and young adults are constructed within the formal reasoning framework. Their focus is on evaluating students' assessment of arguments or statements. They follow a traditional "inventory of thinking skills" approach and their scores overlap considerably with measures of intelligence and academic aptitude. Respondents do not generate thoughts themselves but rather judge the accuracy of assumptions, inferences, and deductions presented in the test.

The most commonly used tests of critical thinking are the *Watson-Glaser Critical Thinking Appraisal* and the *Cornell Critical Thinking Test*. Each of these instruments is examined below.

### *The Watson-Glaser Critical Thinking Appraisal*

The Watson-Glaser Critical Thinking Appraisal (Watson & Glaser, 1980) consists of five subtests: Inference, Recognition of Assumptions, Deduction, Interpretation, and Evaluation of Arguments.

In the following example of an Inference item, students read the passage and indicate whether the statements following it are true, probably true, probably false, false, or whether there is insufficient data to decide.

> Two hundred students in their early teens voluntarily attended a recent weekend student conference in a Midwestern city. At this conference, the topics of race relations and means of achieving lasting world peace were discussed, since they were the problems the students selected as being the most vital in today's world.
>
> 1. As a group, the students who attended this conference showed a keener interest in broad social problems than do most other students in their early teens.
>
> 2. The majority of the students had not previously discussed the conference topics in their schools.
>
> 3. The students came from all sections of the country.

4. The students discussed mainly labor relations problems.

5. Some teenage students felt it worthwhile to discuss problems of race relations and ways of achieving world peace.

From this example, it should be evident that the Watson-Glaser test items are designed within the framework of formal reasoning. Students must decide, from the information given, whether or not the inferences drawn are in accord with the statements. The test takers do not actually draw inferences but rather evaluate the various inferences put before them. Throughout the test there are also no opportunities to recognize assumptions (without prompting), make deductions, formulate interpretations, or evaluate arguments in their own terms. What is missing are opportunities for the test takers to construct their own meanings. This feature is characteristic of all items on the test.

Not only does the test require no constructed answers, but also the opportunities for guessing are quite high. In the above example, the student has one chance in five of obtaining a correct answer by guessing. On the remaining four subtests, the student's choice is restricted even further because items on these subtests offer only two alternatives.

The split-half reliability coefficients for this test range from .69 at Grade 9 to .76 at Grade 12. Correlations with reading ability at Grades 8 and 9 are reported in the manual to be .50 and .51 respectively. Correlations with intelligence, as measured by the Otis-Lennon School Abilities Test, range from .62 to .70.

Although the Watson-Glaser test is the oldest and best established measure of critical thinking, it should be noted that the reported reliability coefficients are quite low and that the only evidence of validity reported in the manual is correlations with measures of school skills and intelligence. There are no correlations with other exercises that purport to measure thinking processes. Further, we have no way of knowing whether the inferences, assumptions, deductions, interpretations, and evaluations to which the students react on the test items reflect thought processes that the student would actually use when confronted by a problem situation.

## *The Cornell Critical Thinking Test*

The Cornell Critical Thinking Test (Ennis, Millman, & Tomko, 1985) is available in two forms, Level X for students in Grades 4 through 14 and Level Z for advanced high school students, college students, and other adults.

In both forms, students are asked to identify instances of good reasoning versus bad reasoning by evaluating statements. The first part of the Level Z test is designed to measure deduction. The first section describes two men debating about the voting age. Arguments are advanced by each man and the student is asked to evaluate each argument using the following alternatives:

A. Conclusion *follows necessarily* from the statements.
B. Conclusion *contradicts* the statements given.
C. *Neither*

The arguments are presented in a point-counterpoint context:

1. Mr. Wilstings says that eighteen-year olds haven't faced the problems of the world, and that anyone who hasn't faced these problems shouldn't vote. What he says is correct, but eighteen-year olds still should be able to vote. They're mature human beings, aren't they?

2. Furthermore, eighteen-year olds should be allowed to vote because anyone who will suffer or gain from a decision made by the voters ought to be permitted to vote. It is clear that eighteen-year olds will suffer or gain from the decision made by the voters.

Eight similar statements complete Section one. The remaining sections are titled Semantics, Credibility (of statements), Induction, Definition Identification, and Assumption Identification.

Level X is the more attractive of the two forms of The Cornell Critical Thinking Test. This form consists of 71 test items connected by a story line that runs through all of the questions. The story describes the activities of a search party that has arrived on the planet of Nicoma to find out what has happened to a group of explorers who were sent to the planet earlier and who are now missing. Members of the search party make observations, advance hypotheses, hear reports from their experts, and interpret evidence. Students answer multiple-choice questions designed to measure whether or not the information bears on the hypotheses, whether or not the information is reliable, whether or not the statements made by the explorers follow the premises, and whether or not certain assumptions are made.

The reliability for Level X is higher than for Level Z. The Kuder-Richardson reliabilities for Level X range from .67 to .90 at the 8th-grade level and range from .77 to .81 at the 12-grade level. Support for the validity of the test is offered in the test manual by a number of correlations with school ability and achievement, ranging from a low of .27 with the nonlanguage section of the California Test of Mental Maturity to a high of .74 with the Otis-Lennon School Abilities Test.

Although the reliability of the Cornell test, particularly that of Level Z, is satisfactory, the validity data include no evidence that the tests actually measure thinking processes. The Cornell test, in common with the Watson-Glaser test, elicits no original thinking from respondents but obtains only evaluations of thought processes presented in the test items.

Messick (1984) makes an important distinction between tests of "maximal" performance and tests of "typical" performance. The first type of test measures what an individual *can* do. The second type of test measures what an individual is *likely* to do. We can see that items on the Watson-Glaser and Cornell tests may measure the student's ability to perform inductive and deductive processes when prompted. However, there is no assurance that individuals who do well on these tests will actually use similar reasoning when confronted with everyday reasoning situations.

Siegel (1988) stresses the importance of the "critical spirit" as a determinate of what a student is likely to do when faced with complexity and identifies the disposition to be a critical thinker as an important component of thinking behavior.

> Critical thinking extends far beyond skills of statement assessment, and centrally includes certain dispositions, habits of mind, and (even) character traits; and the disposition to be a critical thinker - that is, the disposition to utilize appropriate criteria in the evaluation of statements and actions, and to value belief and action which is guided by reasons - is perhaps the most important "non-skill" component of critical thinking. (p. 7)

In summary, the Watson-Glaser and Cornell tests measure students' assessment of arguments or statements. The subtests reflect a traditional *inventory of thinking skills* approach and their scores overlap with measures of academic aptitude and achievement. Test takers do not construct interpretations themselves but rather judge the accuracy of interpretations and judgments presented in the test. In addition, these tests do not take into account the disposition to think critically.

### *The Ennis-Weir Critical Thinking Essay Test*

An attempt has been made to formulate a test in which students have more freedom in evaluating arguments and assessing statements. In The Ennis-Weir Critical Thinking Essay Test, the student constructs a response to arguments advanced in a "letter to the editor."

This test consists of a letter written to the editor of a newspaper. Each of the eight short paragraphs of the letter gives a reason or reasons supporting the idea of prohibiting parking between 2 a.m. and 6 a.m., thus eliminating all overnight parking. The introductory paragraph reads as follows (Ennis & Weir, 1985):

> For one thing, to park overnight is to have a garage in the streets. Now it is illegal for anyone to have a garage in the city streets. Clearly, then, it should be against the law to park overnight in the streets.

Test takers write a paragraph in reply to each given paragraph telling whether they believe the thinking is good or bad. They also write a closing paragraph considering the letter as a total argument. They are to include reasons and defenses of judgments. The test manual presents a discussion of each paragraph and directions for scoring. Some reasons get more points than others. On the next page of the manual is a typical discussion of how to grade a particular answer, as in the following example:

> In the light of these faults, the letter writer's failure to say where people would park their cars at night if they did not park them in the streets is a comparatively unimportant defect of the argument of Paragraph One.
>
> It is conceivable, though unlikely, that a respondent might argue effectively that there are important or relevant similarities between parking in the streets and having a garage in the streets (for example, occupying land). Because the ways in which they are similar are, presumably, not against the law, only partial credit (up to two points) should be given someone defending this aspect of the paragraph's argument. (p. 12)

There are no validity data presented in the test manual and virtually no reliability data. The test has been tried out on 55 students, 27 undergraduates in an introductory informal logic class and 28 gifted eighth graders who have received critical thinking instruction. A mean score of 23.8 for undergraduates and 18.6 for eighth graders was obtained. Interrater reliability is reported as .86 and .82 respectively.

Ennis and Weir claim this is a real-world test and state, "Arguments in the real world require considerable interpretation (in context), require evaluation of the content as well as form, often have value dimensions, and do not have mechanical decision procedures" (p. 3).

The authors further claim that one of the key qualities of their test is recognition of values and creative elements in critical thinking ability. It is hard to ascertain how an individual could include values or be very creative in responding without being punished for it by the scoring system. In fact, the test is criticized by Rudman (1985) as being too mechanical. Even this attempt by Ennis and Weir to provide for original constructions by students rests on the assumption that thinking is primarily a process of conforming to prescribed rules of logical reasoning.

# 2

# *Thinking as Levels of Cognitive Complexity*

Whether or not constructive thought proceeds as a progression of logical sequences is open to question. William James' (1880) early descriptions of thought processes, particularly higher thought processes, seems consistent with more recent conceptions of creative thought. According to James:

> Instead of thoughts of concrete things patiently following one another in a beaten track of habitual suggestion, we have the most abrupt cross-cuts and transitions from one idea to another, the most rarified abstractions and discriminations, the most unheard-of combinations of elements, the subtlest associations of analogy; in a word, we seem suddenly introduced into a seething caldron of ideas, where everything is fizzling and bobbling about in a state of bewildering activity, where partnerships can be joined or loosened in an instant, treadmill routine is unknown, and the unexpected seems the only law...the same premises would not, in the mind of another individual, have engendered just that conclusion; although, when the conclusion is offered to the other individual, he may thoroughly accept and enjoy it, and envy the brilliancy of him to whom it first occurred. (p. 185)

This quotation suggests that thinking is marked less by conscious inductive and deductive reasoning than by more diffuse associative and elaborative processes. The extent to which individual differences in such cognitive processes operate in the perception and interpretation of reality is illustrated by the following paragraphs, which we collected from university students. These were written after observing a German helmet from World War II and an American helmet from World War I displayed simultaneously.

1. Two helmets: Both are circular in shape and dark in color. One helmet is brown: while the other appears to be black. Both helmets seem to be antique and made from a hard metal, probably iron.

   Although the two helmets are similar in some ways, they are very different. They seem to represent two different ideas. Perhaps they were the helmets of two opposing sides during a war long ago. Its also possible that they represent two different time periods. It seems too obvious that there is some historical link between the helmets.

   One helmet has a chin strap and the other does not. One has a brim all the way around: while the other has only a front brim. Both have padding on the inside, probably for comfort more than anything else. One of the helmets has bolts in the sides; the other does not. One helmet comes down over the ears and neck, probably provides more protection where the other does not. Both helmets are rusting. Both are outdated. Both are inflexible. (S.L)

2. Two helmets rest side by side on a table. The dark, old relics of past wars seem to have been lovingly kept through many years. Do they remind their owner of bravery in enemy land? Do they seek to still testify loyalty to the United States-a loyalty so deep that one's life is risked and one dares to travel far to fight for freedom? Or perhaps they bear a solemn tribute to the

> perils and heartaches of war and to men who never came back home.
>
> Now they rest, silently and forlornly on a table. The wars for which they were made have long since ended. War now seems to belong to other places and other times. To young citizens they appear as curiosities-mementos for a history buff collection or as part of a museum display. To older citizens they stir memories of an era long ago. They have a story to be told-and something important to share with people today. Maybe they will prompt someone to tell it. (J.J.)

These examples illustrate the dramatic differences in the way two people perceive and construct reality. In this open-ended exercise, we can see the process of the individual structuring the situation. The primary task of researchers attempting to measure thinking is to describe more fully the processes by which individuals perceive and construct interpretations of problem situations, situations marked by uncertainty, ambiguity, and the absence of a preformed response.

We turn now to the work of other researchers who have investigated thinking processes that occur when individuals try to make sense of situations that are open to a variety of interpretations.

### *The Describer–Explainer Continuum*

Peel (1971) felt that to observe thinking it was necessary to ask for explanations. Low-level thinking was characterized by simple descriptions. High-level thinking made use of cause-and-effect explanations. Thinking was further evaluated by the way the problem was perceived, the generality of concepts brought to bear, and the ability to imagine alternatives. Peel stressed the individual's ability to use personal knowledge to construct possible explanations not clearly present in the situation. According to Peel:

> The distinction between content-dominated answers and imaginative responses invoking explanations is crucial in this study of adolescent thinking. . .. The transition from content-dominated to possibility evoking answers seemed to be the predominant feature of early and mid-adolescent thinking. (p. 26)

Peel (1971) described a number of exercises designed to elicit understandings and judgments from students. In an exercise originally developed by Rhys (1964), students read an account of an Andean farmer who cut down the forest and planted a crop that produced a profitable harvest. Other farmers followed his example. Soon floods eroded the soil and the land became barren. After reading the story, students responded to the question, "Why did the deep fertile soil cover disappear and make farming impossible?"

Student responses were scored on a describer/explainer continuum. Low scores represent simple description and repetition of the information given without reference to other ideas, analogies, similarities, or antecedent or contiguous circumstances. High scores reflect use of cause-and-effect relationships and world knowledge in constructing explanations. Phenomena are causally connected to previous phenomena and independent generalizations.

Individuals who respond to story situations with concrete descriptions are limited to a recapitulation of the givens of the situation. In such cases, the explanations amount to little more than descriptions. They bring little in the way of abstract concepts, comparisons, evaluations, or analytic insights to the problem. Higher level thinkers see causal connections and draw on their own knowledge of how things work in the world to generate alternate explanations.

### *Perry's Positions of Intellectual Development*

Among the landmark studies of intellectual development is the work of William Perry (1970) based on interviews with students at Harvard University. Perry proposed a scheme of developmental stages that characterize the shifts in thinking patterns from the freshman to the senior year. Overall, the student moves from viewing the world as a series of right/wrong categories to an understanding that decisions and commitments must be made in a world marked by uncertainty and incomplete information.

In Perry's description of his nine levels of intellectual development, he capitalized such words as *Absolute* and *Answers* to indicate the prominent role such concepts play in the cognitive processes of the thinker. The nine developmental positions, which characterize the development of intellectual maturity, are as follows:

> Position 1: The student sees the world in polar terms of we-right-good vs. other-wrong-bad. Right Answers for everything exist in the Absolute, known to Authority whose role is to mediate (teach) them. Knowledge and goodness are perceived as quantitative accretions of discrete rightness to be collected by hard work and obedience (paradigm: a spelling test).
>
> Position 2: The student perceives diversity in opinion, and uncertainty, and accounts for them as unwarranted confusion in poorly qualified Authorities or as mere exercises set by Authority "so we can learn to find The Answer for ourselves."
> Position 3: The student accepts diversity and uncertainty as legitimate but still temporary in areas where Authority "hasn't found the Answer yet." He supposes Authority grades him in these areas on "good expression" but remains puzzled as to standards.

Position 4: (a) The student perceives legitimate uncertainty (and therefore diversity of opinion) to be extensive and raises it to the status of an unstructured epistemological realm of its own in which he sets over against Authority's realm where right-wrong still prevails, or (b) the student discovers qualitative contextual relativistic reasoning as a special case of "what They want" within Authority's realm.

Position 5: The student perceives all knowledge and values (including authority's) as contextual and relativistic and subordinates dualistic right-wrong functions to the status of a special case, in context.

Position 6: The student apprehends the necessity of orienting himself in a relativistic world through some form of personal Commitment (as distinct from unquestioned or unconsidered commitment to simple belief in certainty).

Position 7: The student makes an initial Commitment in some area.

Position 8: The student experiences the implications of Commitment, and explores the subjective and stylistic issues of responsibility.

Position 9: The student experiences the affirmation of identity among multiple responsibilities and realizes Commitment as an ongoing, unfolding activity through which he expresses his life style. (pp. 9 &10)

Perry brings to the forefront structural considerations, an individual's expectations about the world, and his procedures for making sense of experiences. In Perry's words, *structure* refers to "the formal properties of the assumptions and expectancies a person holds at a given time in regard to the nature and origins of knowledge and value" (p. 42).

Perry's work is particularly relevant to our efforts in two ways:

1. It provides some of the "marker characteristics" that help distinguish less mature from more mature thinking.

2. It strengthens the argument that fundamental psychological processes mediate thinking in free situations, perhaps much more powerfully than do the rules of right reasoning.

Certainly, the idea of mental schemata influencing the perception and interpretation of the world has been around in some form or other since William James, with Bartlett and Piaget elaborating this concept in the context of empirical work. Perry's work, however, provides data with college-age students illustrating the transition from an early need to simplify the world to a later acceptance of a more uncertain world of complex interpretations.

### *Information Processing Structures*

The work of Perry is related to the work of Harvey, Hunt, and Schroder (1961), who independently arrived at similar formulations of the way an individual's conceptual system mediates the perception of and interactions with the environment. Schroder, Driver, and Streufert (1967) build on these conceptions of an information processing view of thinking, to which we now turn.

Within the information processing framework, attitudes, needs, strategies, concepts, and norms are seen as information processing *structures*, which function in differentiating the environment and integrating perceptions into beliefs and actions. Individuals with more complex cognitive structures are able to see more dimensions in a stimulus array (works of art, nations, etc.) and are able to make finer distinctions among them. Through these processes, elements of the environment take on *dimensional values*. "Information processing refers to the nature and interdependence of conceptual rules available for organizing dimensional values" (Schroder et al., p. 14).

The differentiation of the environment into many parts and the discrimination of each part into fine distinctions are not enough to assure more adaptive thinking. These perceived elements might be combined in simplistic ways. On the other hand, given more complex combinatory rules, the potential for generating new attributes of information and making more connections is enhanced. Thus, the *level of integrative complexity* is a key concept in their scheme of analysis. According to Schroder et al., individuals with a low integration index would be expected to exhibit the following thinking processes:

1. Categorical, black & white thinking.
2. Minimization of conflict.
3. The anchoring of behavior in external conditions.
4. Abrupt and compartmentalized shifts in categorizations.

As individuals move into somewhat higher levels of conceptual integration, the system becomes less determinate and is able to generate alternative organizations. Behaviors associated with the second level of cognitive complexity are as follows:

1. Movement away from absolutism.
2. Emergence of primitive internal causation.
3. Ambivalence and lack of consistency in decision making.
4. Dominance of one perceptual organization over alternative organizations.
5. A "pushing against" present or alternative schemas.

At the moderately high level of integrative complexity, more dimensions are generated, discrimination between stimuli becomes more linear, the person is able to combine schemata, and more alternatives are generated and examined before decisions are made. The behavioral characteristics associated with this level of integration are as follows:

1. A less deterministic system.

2. The simultaneous perception of the situation from two points of view.
3. Greater use of internal processes in generating possibilities.

At high levels of integrative complexity, it is possible to generate or apply general laws that systematize a large and differentiated body of information. The difference between moderately high and high levels may be loosely described as the difference between an empirical and a theoretical outlook. There is an increased potential for the structure to generate alternate patterns of interactions and new schemata.

This description of the information processing structures points to cognitive structures or rules for making meaning and generating knowledge that lie on a continuum ranging from simplistic categorization and evaluation of information to the ability to generate theoretical frameworks that organize complex events and relations.

Peel, Perry, and Schroder et al. have provided the basic concepts we have used in constructing interpretive exercises and scoring procedures for evaluating levels of thinking.

3

# *Interpretive Exercises and The Scoring Rationale for Evaluating Levels of Thinking*

## Interpretive Exercises

We have produced and collected data on two interpretive exercises, The Holocaust and the Bomb Factories. Each of these exercises presents students with a complex situation and asks for their written interpretations.

### *The Holocaust*

The Holocaust exercise consists of a 14-minute video tape and four pages of printed material about the mass killing of Jews by the Nazi government. The video tape is a condensed version of the 1-hour film, *Genocide* (Simon Wiesenthal Center). The tape presents background information about the conditions in Germany following World War I, focusing on the unemployment and loss of self-esteem. The need for a scapegoat is linked with Hitler's campaign of harassment of the Jews. The tape includes scenes of life in the ghettos, the killing of Jewish civilians behind the lines, the transports, and the atrocities of the concentration camps. The printed material provides additional details about some of the major themes introduced in the film. Both the tape and the written material provide students with information that can be used in developing a relatively complex view of the Holocaust.

Following the presentation of the material, students write answers to five questions that provide broad opportunities to organize and interpret the material, for example, "Could a tragedy like this one happen again? What are the reasons for your answer?" The exercise is not timed. Students spend from 10 to 30 minutes answering all five questions.

The scoring rationale directs attention to the way the individual perceives, organizes, and constructs explanations. The scoring of the question "Could a tragedy like this one happen again?" illustrates the scoring procedure. The guiding idea in scoring student responses was to detect the level of cognitive complexity reflected in the answers.

At the low end of the scale, this turned out to be remarkably easy. A number of students quickly simplified the situation into a "good guy/bad guy" dichotomy, reflecting Perry's lowest developmental level, a tendency to see the world in terms of black/white, right/wrong categories. For example, typical Level 1 responses exhibited interpretations in terms of simple absolutes, as in the following:

> "No, I don't believe this will ever happen again. I'm sure if something as inhumane as this started to happen the U. S. will step in and stop it."

> "No, I don't think anybody but Hitler could possibly hate a certain group of people as he did."

At the second level, we searched for some indication that the student was attempting to build a causal network by bringing in at least one reason to support a position, that is the emergence of Peel's explainer. Examples are as follows:

> "I think people today value human life more. If this did reoccur, I believe it would be stopped once someone knew what was going on."

> "Yes, small countries whose leaders are picked without the people's consent would probably have a better chance of this happening."

At the third level, the network of causation contains at least two elements, and the explanations reflect some of the contingencies that surrounded Hitler's rise to power, such as the indifference of other nations and the internal conditions in Germany that made a strong leader welcome. The following are examples of the third level:

> "I think that the memory of the Holocaust will live forever, and people will be on the look-out for rising leaders such as Hitler. Foreign countries would probably intervene much quicker if a situation like this happened again."

> "Yes, if a society is having a very bad situation, a great new leader with an idea that seems wonderful comes along, then it seems entirely possible that they would follow him/her and do exactly as they instruct."

At Level 4, there is more elaboration of the supporting ideas (as opposed to simple listing of reasons). In addition, we can observe below in the second example the introduction of world knowledge that is not contained in the original presentation of the problem. The following are examples of the fourth level:

> "No, I don't believe a tragedy on this scale could happen again. There are too many checks and balances between countries and their citizens for this to happen again. No country is faced with the same problems Germany was faced with back then. (At least not to the same extent.) There is no reason for this to happen again. I also believe that hindsight will help our (and

> other nation's) foresight. I don't believe that any nation would stand for this happening again."

> "I don't think so. Well, then, again, possibly. People are being killed daily by governments and government enforcers, not on such a large scale. I think that economic sanctions and trade embargoes could pressure a country in today's world not to do something that silly."

At Level 5, responses exhibited a network of causation that synthesized information and led to more global and integrated assessments. Outside analogies or parallels with current events were employed to elucidate the situation.

> "As an eternal optimist, I hope that this could never happen again. However, what has been done in 40 years to change humans from allowing another Holocaust from happening? The same reasons of fear, depression, and prejudice have not been taken away from our society. People always want someone to blame. Whether it is the witches in Salem during the 1700's or Communists in Washington during the 1950's, we often take our fears and act viciously because of them. Until we are truly able to accept different people and ideas, there will still be the slight possibility that it could happen again."

> "I suppose it would be possible for such a tragedy to reoccur, but it would not do so in a country that had been a democracy for a long time. In a democracy, people are too involved in their government to let a dictator take over. In a country ravaged by hunger, poverty, unemployment, and depression, people will look to someone to help them. It that person is a dictator, and the people are use to dictators, he will not have much of a problem getting into power. When coming into or during control of a country, a person needs to find a scapegoat. It could be an abstract emotion, such as fear, or a race, such as the Jews. In a country suffering greatly, the people will look for a way out. The way out may be a leader like Hitler, and another Holocaust might begin."

A fuller description of The Holocaust and the scoring rationale has been presented by McDaniel & Thompson (1989). Data collected from 153 eighth-grade students revealed correlations of .45 with the total score of the California Achievement Test (1985), .44 with grades in history, .35 with learner autonomy, and .26 with task involvement. All of these correlations are significant ($p <$ .01, one-tailed test).

The scoring of responses to The Holocaust provided the first iteration of the scoring rationale, which was further developed in the second interpretive exercise described below. The scoring reflected a continuum ranging from attention to trivial factual detail at the lower end to recognition of causal relationships and complexities at the upper end.

### *The Bomb Factories*

The Bomb Factories exercise consists of a 14-minute video tape edited from an American Broadcasting Corporation (ABC) news presentation and two pages of readings excerpted from *Time* magazine. The tape and the readings describe problems with plant safety and environmental pollution from nuclear waste. There are reports of cancer and thyroid problems caused by exposure to toxic materials within the plant and in the immediate environment. The tape presents viewpoints of government officials, plant managers, safety inspectors, workers, and nearby residents.

After viewing the tape and reading the excerpt, students are instructed as follows: "You have just seen a tape and read a magazine article about The Bomb Factories. Tell us what you think about this situation. Take a few minutes to reflect on what you have heard and seen. Take your time, describe and explain your thoughts as completely and fully as possible." Student responses range in length from one sentence to one-and-one-half pages of handwritten material. These responses are evaluated with the aid of a scoring rationale.

## The Scoring Rationale for Evaluating Levels of Thinking

The scoring rationale is designed to provide an index of the cognitive complexity reflected in the responses of the students. The rationale directs the attention of the scorer to three aspects of the student's response: a). the way problem situations are perceived and defined, b). the way an organizing structure is developed, and c). the way positions are analyzed, supported, and elaborated. Each of these strands is presented in more detail below.

### *Perception and Definition of the Situation*

This strand describes the way the student represents or encodes the situation. Rarely is all of the information used. The student perceives and selects salient features to characterize the situation and give it meaning. The student's initial perceptions define the complexity seen in the issues presented. The representation of the problem sets the limits and opens the possibilities for further elaboration and analysis.

At the lower end of the strand, the student simplifies the situation and ignores information. At the upper end of the strand, the student preserves the complexity in the situation and incorporates divergent information.

### *Imposition of an Organizing Structure*

This strand describes the construction of an organizing structure that helps make sense of the situation and provides a basis for interpretations. This structure includes a frame of reference within which the events are interpreted. This frame of reference reflects the student's values, concerns, and world knowledge.

Additionally, the interpretations of the situation are constructed around certain organizing ideas, or nodes. The organizing ideas may be relatively narrow and fact-like or broader and more inclusive. Imposing a simple structure (conventional framework, few nodes, narrow concepts) leads to superficial and obvious interpretations. Imposing a complex structure (interpretive framework, many nodes, broad concepts) leads to deeper analysis and integrated, comprehensive interpretations.

At the lower end of the strand, the student accepts and simplifies the framework explicitly provided. The interpretation employs narrowly defined concepts and few nodes. The student adds no new ideas or perspectives. At the upper end, the student extends the framework, bringing in world knowledge and value positions not implied by the situation. The interpretation is built around broad concepts which facilitate reorganizing, restructuring and reconceptualizing the problem situation.

### *Analysis, Support, and Elaboration*

This strand describes the way the student analyzes the situation and supports a position. The progression from low to high is marked by a shift from descriptions to explanations. Describing is characterized by restatements of the given information coupled with assertions rather than reasons. Explaining is characterized by an integrated network of relationships.

At the lower end of the strand, the student paraphrases information and uses assertions, simple rules, and appeals to authority. At the upper end, the student constructs networks of casual relationships, applies principles, uses analogies, generalizes, and extrapolates.

These strands are used by scorers in deciding which of five levels of thinking to assign any given student's response. These levels are described next.

### *Levels of Cognitive Complexity*

Level 1: Unilateral Descriptions

The students: Simplifies the situation. Focuses on one idea or argument. Does not identify alternatives. Brings in no new information, meaning, or perspectives. Makes good/bad and either/or assertions. Appeals to authority or simple rules. Simply paraphrases, restates or repeats information.

Level 2: Simplistic Alternatives

Identifies simple and obvious conflicts, but the conflicts are not pursued or analyzed. Develops a position by dismissing or ignoring one alternative and supporting the other with assertions and simple explanations rather than by making a deeper assessment of the situation.

Level 3: Emergent Complexity

The Student: Identifies more than one possible explanation or perspective. Establishes and preserved complexity. Introduces new elements. Supports position through comparisons and simple causal statements.

Level 4: Broad Interpretations

The student: Uses broad ideas to help define and interpret the situation. Manipulates ideas within the perspective established. Has a clearly recognizable explanatory theme. Integrates ideas into "subassemblies," each supporting a component of the explanation.

Level 5: Integrated Analysis

The student: Restructures or reconceptualizes the situation and approaches the problem from a new point of view. Constructs a network of cause-and-effect relationships. Integrates and extrapolates ideas. Arrives at new interpretations by analogy, application of principles, generalizations, and world knowledge. Constructs an organizing framework, sketches connections, and predicts consequences.

# 4

# *Empirical Studies*

The reliability of the scoring procedure was determined by computing a correlation coefficient between the independent ratings of each of the authors for a sample of 39 answer sheets drawn randomly from a sample of 78 eleventh grade students enrolled in social studies classes in a high school serving a university community (School E below). The inter-rater reliability indicated by this procedure was .80.

## Experimental Groups

During the spring of 1989, The Bomb Factories was administered to 502 students from the 5th-grade through the college graduate level. The characteristics of the schools involved were as follows:

School A: metropolitan, inner city, gifted students, elementary school.
School B: urban, university community, middle school.
School C: rural, consolidated, middle school.
School D: rural/urban, consolidated, high school.
School E: urban, university community, high school.

The means (*M*), standard deviations (*SD*) and ranges obtained at various grade levels are displayed in Table 4-1.

Table 4-1. Means, Standard Deviations, and Ranges of Levels of Thinking at Various Educational Levels on The Bomb Factories

| School | grade | n | *M* | *SD* | range |
|---|---|---|---|---|---|
| A | 5 | 24 | 1.46 | .64 | 1-3 |
| B | 8 | 42 | 2.02 | .88 | 1-4 |
| C | 8 | 190 | 2.27 | .84 | 1-4 |
| D | 11 | 32 | 2.70 | .95 | 1-5 |
| E | 11 | 78 | 2.93 | .99 | 1-5 |
| Undergraduate | | | | | |
| Teacher Ed | | 53 | 2.23 | 1.09 | 1-5 |
| Art Ed | | 51 | 1.92 | .87 | 1-5 |
| Graduate | | | | | |
| Education | | 32 | 2.26 | 1.01 | 1-5 |

From the data in Table 1, it is evident that the mean Level of thinking, as measured by The Bomb Factories, exhibits a progressive increase from grade five through grade eleven. The college samples do not reflect additional increments, but these data were obtained from class projects conducted by students who had no previous experience using the scoring rationale, and we are not certain to what extent this factor influenced the mean scores.

One may also observe that no one in the fifth grade attained a thinking level higher than 3, at the eighth grade, no one achieved a level of 5, and at high school and college levels, the full range of levels is represented. These data suggest that the performance on The Bomb Factories is related, as we might expect, to developmental levels as indicated by grade placement, at least through the high school years.

### *School Achievement Variables*

We have investigated the relationship of levels of thinking with a number of indices of school achievement. Table 4-2 presents the correlations that were found between level of thinking and the school achievement variables: course grades, a history essay grade, and standardized achievement scores. The standardized achievement test used in this study was the Indiana State Test for Educational Progress (ISTEP). This test is essentially a replica of The California Achievement Test (McGraw-Hill, 1985). The history essay grade was the teacher's grade assigned to student responses to three questions related to the Civil War.

Table 4-2. Correlations Among Grades, Standardized Achievement Tests, and Levels of Thinking on The Bomb Factories

| | Grade 8 | Grade 11 | |
|---|---|---|---|
| | School C n=54 | School D n=18 | School E n=78 |
| Semester Grades | | | |
| English | .27 | – | – |
| History | .39** | .57** | .37** |
| Science | .30* | – | – |
| Mathematics | .20 | – | – |
| History Essay Grade | – | – | .22* |
| ISTEP Achievement Subtests | | | |
| Vocabulary | .38** | – | – |
| Reading Comp | .26* | – | – |
| Spelling | .15 | – | – |
| Language Mech | .07 | – | – |
| Language Exp | .36** | – | – |
| Math Comp | .14 | – | – |
| Math Concepts | .22 | – | – |
| Study Skills | .21 | – | – |
| Science | .35** | – | – |
| Social Studies | .31* | – | – |
| Reading Total | .40** | – | – |
| Language Total | .26* | – | – |
| Math Total | .29* | – | – |

*$p < .05$, **$p < .01$ *(All probabilities reported in this study are one-tailed)*

To what extent does performance on The Bomb Factories reflect general student achievement? With the exception of the single correlation of .57 between semester grades in history and levels of thinking, scores on The Bomb Factories reach only moderate levels of correlations with measures of school achievement. The highest correlation with achievement test scores is with the total reading score of the ISTEP (.40). Scores for vocabulary, science, language expression, and history grades are also significantly correlated ($p < .01$) with The Bomb Factories. Although five additional correlations in Table 4-2 are significant at the .05 level, they tend to be lower, none of them exceeding a magnitude of .31. Taken together, these correlations with grades and achievement test scores suggest that performance on The Bomb Factories is moderately related to general school achievement.

The magnitude of the correlations among levels of thinking and school achievement seem about right. If the correlations were consistently high (.65 or above) an argument could be made that scores on The Bomb Factories reflect little more than general school achievement. On the other hand, if the correlations were consistently low we would find it difficult to explain how a measure of thinking could be unrelated to other indices of school performance. In any event, it should be clear that measures of school achievement represent variables that are conveniently collected, but play only a minor role in validating measures of thinking. Their primary relevance is their use in demonstrating that a new measure purporting to measure thinking is not simply some variant of a test of general ability, nor overly susceptible to such school skills as reading ability or achievement in social studies and science. The low-to-moderate correlation coefficients presented in Table 4-2 suggest that The Bomb Factories is neither unrelated to conventional academic performance nor unduly influenced by typical school proficiencies.

***Relationship to Writing Proficiency***

Since The Bomb Factories and The Holocaust both employ written responses of students, it is reasonable to ask to what extent writing skills are related to scores on these interpretive exercises. For the two 11th-grade classes in our studies, students had also been administered a writing assessment exercise as part of the ISTEP. All writing samples from the ISTEP were evaluated by trained scorers on four dimensions using a scale of 1 to 6. Each of these dimensions and the extreme points on the scales, as defined in the report to students, are discussed below.

1. Holistic. Evaluates the student's writing as a whole on a scale ranging from (1) "seriously deficient" to (6) "exceptionally proficient."

2. Analytic Focus. Evaluates the focus of the student's writing. Evaluations range from (1) "main point lacking; no control of topic, point-of-view, or language" to (6) "main point clearly stated; strong, consistent point-of-view; effective use of language."

3. Organization. Evaluates the organization of the student's writing on a scale from (1) "no organization, transitions, progression, or introduction and conclusion" to (6) "effective organization; superior transitions; smooth progression; effective introduction and conclusion."

4. Development. Evaluates the development of the student's writing from (1) "undeveloped; ideas do not relate to or support the main idea" to (6) "fully elaborated; well-defined main and secondary points supported by rich details and ideas."

Correlations among The Bomb Factories, The Holocaust, and the four scores of the writing assessment task are shown in Table 4-3. For this group, The Holocaust were scored using the scoring rationale used for The Bomb Factories.

The data in table 4-3 indicate that scores on the Bomb Factories are significantly correlated with Focus and Development on the writing assessment for the students in school D.

For School E, however, only the Holistic assessment of the writing sample is significantly correlated with scores on the Bomb Factories exercise. For School E almost identical correlations were obtained when scores on the writing sample were correlated with scores from the Holocaust. Because of the larger number of cases in School E and the replication of results from one interpretive exercise to another, we conclude that there is an association between writing ability as measured by the holistic assessment of writing and scores on levels of thinking. Since the amount of variance in the interpretive exercises explained by this aspect of writing skill would be approximately 19% (the square of the correlation coefficient), writing ability would not be the major contributor to scores on the interpretive exercises.

Table 4-3. Correlations among Writing Assessment Scores with Levels of Thinking on The Bomb Factories and The Holocaust

| | School D n = 18 | School E n = 72 | |
|---|---|---|---|
| | Bomb Factories | Bomb Factories | Holocaust |
| Holistic | .24 | .46** | .42** |
| Focus | .51* | -.04 | -.04 |
| Organization | .34 | .02 | .08 |
| Development | .55** | .13 | .15 |

*p < .05, **p < .01

## ***Orientation to Learning Variables***

In this section, we will discuss the relationship of levels of thinking with various indices of the student's orientation to learning: achievement motivation, learning orientation, learning engagement, learning style, and a thinking survey. Below is a description of the measures used.

1. Achievement Motivation (Nicholls, 1989)

A self-report questionnaire on which students use a Likert scale ranging from strongly agree to strongly disagree to indicate when they feel most successful in school. This questionnaire includes subscales designed to measure the following aspects of achievement motivation:

Work Avoidance. 10 item subscale measuring the tendency to avoid school work and effort. A typical item is: "I feel most successful in school if I don't have to do any work.".

Ego Involvement. 6 item subscale measuring a tendency to evaluate one's performance positively only if it indicates that one's ability is superior to that of others. A typical item is: "I feel most successful if I'm the only one who can answer a question."

Task Orientation. 7-item subscale measuring the tendency to increase one's understanding, to accomplish something not previously done, or to improve one's performance. A typical item is: "I feel most successful in school if I get a new idea about how things work."

2. Need for Cognition Scale (Cacioppo & Petty, 1982)

This is a 34-item scale that measures the tendency to engage in and enjoy thinking. A typical item is: "I really enjoy a task that involves coming up with new solutions to problems."

Whereas the original scale required students to use an 8-point Likert scale asking students to rate the degree to which they agree or disagree with each statement, this research used only a 5-point Likert scale.

3. Learner Autonomy (McDaniel & Ferreyra, 1989)

This is a 30-item rating scale, completed by the teacher, measures student autonomy (the ability to work independently, seek understanding, and monitor one's own learning). Two typical items are: "Expresses independent ideas" and "Goes on to new tasks without direction". For each item the teacher indicates how often (rarely, sometimes, frequently) the student exhibits the behavior.

4. Learning Style (Wood & McDaniel, 1990)

This is a 40-item questionnaire with items selected primarily from Schmeck's self-report questionnaire (Schmeck, Ribich, & Ramanaiah, 1977) measuring "deep processing" and "elaborative processing." Two typical true/false items: "I try to resolve conflicts between the information obtained from different sources" and "I try to relate ideas in one subject to those in others whenever possible."

For the eighth-grade sample, a subset of 22 items was selected based on item analysis of the 40-item form administered to 27 eleventh-grade students.

5. Thinking Survey

This is a 15-item questionnaire constructed for this study to measure habits of reflective thinking and evaluating knowledge. Students respond on a 5-point Likert scale ranging from strongly agree to strongly disagree. Two typical items are: "I like to consider a lot of evidence before making up my mind" and "New ideas about a subject always stimulate my thinking."

**Correlation with Orientation to Learning Variables**

The correlations in Table 4-4 show a consistent and moderate relationship between most of the orientation to learning measures and levels of thinking. The negative correlations between work avoidance and The Bomb Factories support our expectation that students who tend to avoid work do not actively engage in processing information and would therefore not do as well on The Bomb Factories. Similarly, the negative values for ego orientation suggest that students who are working to enhance their position in the group rather than working for internal rewards are not likely to engage in critical thinking.

The remaining measures of learning orientation all capture some aspect of intrinsic motivation toward reflective and analytic approaches to ideas. Scores on these instruments reflect what students say about their own orientations to learning. With a single exception (task involvement at the eighth-grade level), these reports are significantly related to the levels of thinking.

Table 4-4. Correlations Among Orientation to Learning Measures and Level of Thinking on The Bomb Factories

| | Grade 8 School C n = 54 | Grade 11 School D n = 53 | Undergrad |
|---|---|---|---|
| Work Avoidance | -.11 | – | -.11 |
| Ego Orientation | -.31* | – | -.11 |
| Task Involvement | .07 | – | .34** |
| Need for Cognition | – | – | .41** |
| Autonomy | .35** | – | – |
| Learning Style | .33** | .41* (n=18) | – |
| Thinking Survey | – | .37** (n=32) | – |

* $\underline{p} < .05$, ** $\underline{p} < .01$

Students who report that they form links between ideas, feel successful when they solve a difficult problem, and like to analyze ideas achieve higher levels of thinking on The Bomb Factories. Additionally, teachers' ratings of students with respect to their autonomy in learning situations are significantly related to student's performance on The Bomb Factories.

### *Other Measures of Cognitive Ability and Thinking Processes*

To further examine the relationship between levels of thinking as measured by The Bomb Factories and other cognitive abilities, we obtained data from the school records. At the middle-school level, five scores were obtained from the Test of Cognitive Skills (CTB/McGraw-Hill, 1987). The following are brief summaries of the subtests:

A. Sequences: letter and pattern sequences
B. Analogies: visual analogies
C. Memory: delayed memory for narrative detail
D. Verbal Reasoning: verbal problems
E. Total: total score on cognitive skills

For the college sample, the Scholastic Aptitude Test's verbal scores (SATV) and and mathematic scores (SATM) were obtained. In addition to these measures, the Watson-Glaser Critical Thinking Test and the Ennis-Weir Critical Thinking Essay Test, both discussed earlier, were administered to the college sample. The Cornell Critical Thinking Test, Level Z was administered to the graduate group. The correlations among among these tests and levels of thinking are presented in Table 4-5.

From the data in Table 4-5, it may be observed that a relatively high correlation (.39) was obtained between the SATV scores and levels of thinking. The relationship between levels of thinking and the Test of Cognitive Skills revealed a significant correlation only for the Analogies subtest. This subtest makes use of visual rather than verbal analogies and might appropriately be interpreted as an index of general ability. This finding, together with the relatively high correlation with the verbal score of the Scholastic Aptitude Test, suggests that there is a moderate correlation between general ability and performance on The Bomb Factories.

Table 4-5. Correlations of Levels of Thinking on the Bomb Factories with Other Measures of Thinking and Cognitive Ability

| | Grade 8 School C n=52 | Undergraduate n=53 | Graduate n=32 |
|---|---|---|---|
| Test of Cognitive Skills | | | |
| Sequence | .05 | – | – |
| Analogies | .35* | – | – |
| Memory | .06 | – | – |
| Verbal Reas | .11 | – | – |
| Total | .14 | – | – |
| SAT Verbal | – | .39* | – |
| SAT Math | – | -.06 | – |
| Cornell | – | – | -.08 |
| Watson-Glaser | – | .08 | – |
| Ennis-Weir | – | .45* | – |

*$p < .01$

The correlations between The Bomb Factories and the other widely used tests of critical thinking, the Watson-Glaser and Cornell, are essentially zero. This finding may be interpreted in terms of the markedly different way in which we have conceptualized and measured thinking. Our earlier discussion contrasted the processes of selecting, organizing, and interpreting information with those processes involved in recognizing instances of right reasoning.

The correlation between The Bomb Factories and the more open Ennis-Weir test is .45. It may be remembered that the essays written for the Ennis-Weir test are highly constrained and are scored within a formal logic framework. Thus, the correlation is actually higher than might be expected. Even so, this significant correlation between The Bomb Factories and the Ennis-Weir test supports the general idea that thinking process may be best observed in tasks requiring samples of thinking generated by the students.

### *Correlations with Other Thinking Exercises*

The major problem in validating tests of thinking has been and continues to be the virtual absence of established tests that can serve as criteria measures. It should be obvious that school marks, standardized achievement tests, and other measures of cognitive ability can not be substituted for indices of thinking processes. We have therefore found it necessary to develop other exercises that would capture some of the processes incorporated in our conceptualization of thinking. In Table 4-6, we present correlations among levels of thinking as measured with four such exercises. The first two, the Two Helmets Test and the Jefferson Davis Exercise, are strictly exploratory and in very early stages of development. The last two, The Holocaust and The Mystery of Pearl Harbor, are much more sophisticated and fully developed. Each of these exercises is described below.

### *The Two Helmets Test*

In this exercise, students observe two military helmets, a German helmet from World War II and an American helmet from World War I. Students are instructed to write their reaction to this display. The display remains in view while the students complete their paragraphs. Samples of responses to this exercise have been presented earlier.

The scores on this test are not presented as a measure of thinking. Students' responses were assigned a score of 1 to 5 based on the extent to which their paragraphs reflected description (1) or imaginative elaboration (5). In the two examples presented earlier, the first would be assigned a score of 1. Although the author of this example is keenly observant and his account is rich in detail, it nevertheless is strictly limited to a descriptive account of the display. In contrast, the second example exhibits a rich associative elaboration that goes well beyond the information given. This exercise was administered to 32 graduate students in education. Our expectation was that students showing a tendency for imaginative elaborations would perform better on The Bomb Factories exercise. The correlation coefficient indicating the extent to which this expectation, and subsequently described expectancy, was met is presented in Table 4-6.

### *The Jefferson Davis Exercise* (Armstrong & McDaniel, 1987)

This exercise is essentially a question-asking exercise. Conflicting quotations about Jefferson Davis are presented, and students are asked to write down any questions they would like to pursue and to explain why they asked each question. The questions generated by the students were assigned scores using the following four levels:

A. Questions that ask for simple details that are unrelated to larger issues and not open to interpretation (1 point).

B. Questions that recognize some ambiguity but that can be answered in a simple either/or fashion (2 points).

C. Questions that ask for low-level explanations about narrow content unrelated to larger issues (3 points).

D. Questions that ask for causal relationships and interpretations and attempt to construct larger, general concepts (4 points).

The Jefferson Davis exercise is similar in some ways to The Bomb Factories exercise. Students are confronted with a situation that presents conflicting details and are free to respond in their own individual ways. Some respond by ignoring conflicting information and asking about trivial details. Others appear to be captivated by the ambiguity and ask questions about matters of greater consequence. This exercise was administered to 32 graduate students in education. We expected moderately high correlations between this exercise and the scores on The Bomb Factories.

### *The Holocaust*

This exercise was described earlier. Students watch a video tape and read material describing the ghetto life and mass extermination of European Jews. It is almost a direct parallel to The Bomb Factories, but the answers are generated in response to questions about various aspects of the Holocaust. This exercise was administered to 54 eleventh-grade students in a university community. We expected high correlations between this exercise and The Bomb Factories

### *The Mystery of Pearl Harbor* (Shiang & McDaniel, 1989)

This is a computer-based simulation in which students take the role of a congressional investigator trying to decide who might have been at fault for the complete surprise accompanying the attack on Pearl Harbor. Students examine the exchange of messages between Washington and the military commanders in Hawaii. They also read a description of an intercepted intelligence message and an ignored radar detection of approach planes. They then write summaries presenting their conclusions about who should be blamed for the unpreparedness. Student responses are scored using a scoring rationale similar to that employed for The Bomb Factories. This exercise requires approximately 1 hour to complete. The Pearl Harbor exercise was administered to 18 eleventh-grade students in a consolidated rural/urban high school. We expected a high correlation between the levels of thinking as measured by this exercise and The Bomb Factories.

Table 4-6 presents the correlations among the levels of thinking measured by The Bomb Factories and the scores from the four additional exercises designed to measure related aspects of thinking.

Table 4-6. Correlations Among Levels of Thinking Measured by The Bomb Factories and Other Exercises

| | School D<br>n=18 | School E<br>n=60 | Graduate<br>n=32 |
|---|---|---|---|
| Two Helmets Test | – | – | .26 |
| Jefferson Davis Exercise | – | – | .35* |
| Holocaust | – | .54** | – |
| Pearl Harbor | .65** | – | – |

* *p* < .05, ** *p* < .01

The correlations presented in Table 4-6 represent the most direct evidence we have for the validity of The Bomb Factories as a measure of levels of thinking. All correlations are in the expected direction and the two correlations with the most mature exercises (Holocaust and Pearl Harbor) are among the highest obtained with any of the variables used in this series of studies.

### *Level of Thinking and Discourse Structure*

Additional evidence for the validity of the "Bomb Factories" is presented in a study relating cognitive complexity to discourse structure. Lawrence and Stewart (1990) found a striking continuum of increasing discourse complexity with increasing level of cognitive complexity. Twenty papers from the 72 eleventh grade students responding to the "Bomb Factories" in school E were selected to represent the five levels of cognitive complexity, four papers from each level. These papers were subjected to discourse analysis following the coding instructions described by Cox (1985) which are based on Langer (1986) and theoretical foundations of Halliday's (1985) functional grammar.

Discourse is considered more complex and sophisticated when the following markers are evident. Sophisticated discourse usually has a rhetorical predicate in the top level supported by lexical predicates and other embedded rhetorical predicates at less sophisticated levels discourse might have only lexical predicates used throughout the hierarchy. Rhetorical predicates represent a more global organization while lexical predicates represent local organization. A node indicates a branch point in the discourse structure. Each rhetorical predicate results in at least three nodes and spans two levels in the discourse structure while each lexical predicate results in only one node and spans only one level.

In the table below is a summary of findings at each level of cognitive complexity. Evaluation statements (lexical predicates) are also included since they are used extensively in responses to the "Bomb Factories". In lower level essays, evaluation statements expressing feelings or opinion are used extensively. At higher levels, opinion, feelings, and values are often expressed in more complex causal statements and are classified as rhetorical predicates instead of evaluation/ lexical predicates.

The category for *evaluation statements supported* indicates that the student's evaluation statements were elaborated and supported with *descriptive* or *explanatory* statements. In general this support increases with the increase in Level of Thinking, however at Levels 4 and 5 it begins decreasing. While more evaluations statements overall are used in these Levels, we see a leveling off of the percentage of evaluation statements to the number of nodes and a decrease occurs in the number of supported evaluation statements (the percent expressed is the number of supported evaluation statements divided by the total number of evaluation statements). This occurs because the evaluation statements themselves are also used for support and because other modes of support and elaboration such as examples or time/event series are used.

All frequencies in the table are occurrences within each Level of Thinking (n = 4 papers).

From Table 4-7, we see that the number of sophisticated top structures, rhetorical predicates, increases from one, out of the four papers, at Level 1 to four our of four papers at Levels 3, 4, and 5. An upward trend also occurs in the instances of embedded rhetorical predicates. While there are an equal amount at Levels 2 and 3, at Level 2 the embedded rhetorical predicates are not elaborated upon. At this Level they are statements of minimal causal complexity and commonly occur as a final statement in a line of thought. At Level 3, the embedded rhetorical predicates serve more of a substructure function and are moderately elaborated upon. With Level 4, we see a marked increase in the number of embedded rhetorical predicates. These rhetorical predicates now serve as more fully developed substructures of a unifying theme. It is this aspect of the Level 4 responses which first indicates a more solidified and integrated structure being

Table 4-7. Frequencies of Occurrence of Markers of Sophisticated Discourse at Each Level of Thinking

| Level of Thinking | Rhetorical Predicates Top Structure | Rhetorical Predicates Embedded | Total Nodes | Evaluation Statements | Evaluation Statements Supported |
|---|---|---|---|---|---|
| Level 1 | 1 | 0 | 35 | 20 (57%) | 8 (40%) |
| Level 2 | 2 | 6 | 60 | 20 (33%) | 17 (85%) |
| Level 3 | 4 | 6 | 61 | 18 (29%) | 14 (77%) |
| Level 4 | 4 | 14 | 79 | 22 (28%) | 15 (68%) |
| Level 5 | 4 | 14 | 116 | 36 (31%) | 20 (55%) |

*The above table is excerpted from Lawrence and Stewart (1990).*

formed. While Level 5 responses have the same number of embedded rhetorical predicates, these become broader in context and allow for further connection of ideas within the response. At Level 5 responses, it may also be noticed that there is a large increase in the number of nodes. This increase is indicative of the amount of elaboration and support for each embedded rhetorical predicate. At this level we also see rhetorical predicates embedded within already embedded rhetorical predicates.

The data reported in table 4-7 reveal, for most markers of sophisticated discourse structures, a regular increase in frequency as one examines papers representing progressively higher levels of cognitive complexity.

Taken together, the empirical studies offer strong supporting evidence for the following generalizations. The Bomb Factories provides a measure of thinking processes that is moderately related to general ability and to indices of school achievement. The scores are consistently related to students' self-reports indicating a reflective and analytic engagement with ideas and school subjects. This open-ended measure of thinking shows no relationship to widely recognized multiple-choice measures of critical thinking constructed within the formal logic conceptual framework. The scores show a moderate correlation to critical thinking tests employing student generated answers scored within a formal logic framework. It shows relatively high correlations to other exercises designed to measure thinking processes where such processes are observed through student-generated responses to complex situations and scored for cognitive complexity. Finally, there's a striking continuum of increasing discourse complexity with increasing levels of cognitive complexity.

## Generalizing the Cognitive Complexity Approach

The core of the cognitive complexity approach to thinking processes is the manner in which thinking has been conceptualized and operationalized. The scoring rationale that has been presented represents a means for quantifying student interpretations of complex situations. This scoring rationale is sufficiently general to be applicable to a wide variety of stimulus material. Other investigators may want to select or develop stimulus situations that are open to a variety of interpretations. Schroder et al. (1967) suggest several possibilities for measuring cognitive complexity: present students with uncertainty or conflict, express a point of view and ask students to consider their agreement or disagreement with it, present two discrepant points of view or a number of new ideas and ask students to consider their interrelationships.

We have applied the scoring rationale to other stimulus material, asking students to write their own interpretations of the situation. We have shown the first 28 minutes of "Inside the Jury Room" (PBS Frontline video, 1987). This video shows a jury pondering the fate of a man who has broken the law, but there are extenuating circumstances. In scoring the productions, we found almost all scores falling between the range of Levels 2 and 4 of cognitive complexity. Although initially this film seemed to offer sufficient complexity, it actually led students to a limited number of restricted alternatives. Almost all students saw that within a strict interpretation of the law the defendant was guilty but that his limited mental capacity and the absence of any malicious intent suggested leniency. This example illustrates the difficulty in finding problem situations that are genuinely open to a variety of interpretations and that allow opportunities for students to bring their world knowledge to bear in defining the problem and developing positions. Thus, although the scoring rationale may be applied to a wide range of stimulus materials, care must be taken that the material itself is actually open to formulating interpretive frameworks.

The problem situations and the scoring rationale described in this monograph have been developed primarily as research instruments. Research in the area of thinking skills and cognitive processes has been severely handicapped by the virtual absence of tests of demonstrated validity. We believe that the approach to a conceptualization of measuring thinking processes described in this report will help meet the needs of researchers in this area.

The exercises also have potential as instructional materials. Teachers using these materials have a ready means of engaging students in thinking processes. Students can come to see thinking as a constructive process involving perceiving, formulating, interpreting, and further exploring problem situations. Teachers can provide relatively precise feedback to help students see the nature of their present levels of thinking and to set goals that will help them move through their "zone of proximal development" (Vygotsky, 1962) to higher levels of cognitive complexity.

We have presented in Appendix A the scoring rationale together with specific examples of students writing that illustrate the various levels of cognitive complexity. This scoring rationale was developed by analyzing the responses of the 72 eleventh-grade students in School E. We have included a brief discussion of the salient features that led us to place the writing at a particular level.

It may be important to remember that our samples of students included a high school in a university community and we are inclined to believe that some of the Level 5 responses reflect writing that may be considered "high 5s." Still these examples illustrate the defining characteristics of responses to be scored at that level.

In Appendix B, we have supplied 10 samples of student writing that may be scored by individuals who have familiarized themselves with the scoring rationale. Our scoring of these is presented immediately following the writing samples. Appendix C is a facsimile of the response form we have used in collecting data from the interpretive exercises. Some of our colleagues have suggested that the instructions should be more explicit in requesting a full and complete analysis of the situation. The instructions may reflect the researcher's objectives, that is whether the goal is to measure maximum performance or typical performance. In any event, the demand characteristics built into the directions and the testing situation as a whole are important variables for future research.

The policies of ABC do not permit editing of its video materials. For this reason, other researchers and teachers interested in using The Bomb Factories may want to show the tape in its entirety (approximately 1 hour). Where a shorter testing time is desirable, the first 15 minutes of the tape forms a complete segment illustrating the problems associated with the production of nuclear material at the Fernald plant near Cincinnati.

As mentioned earlier, the studies reported in this monograph employed printed material to supplement the video displays. We are now persuaded that the use of the printed supplements complicates the test procedure unnecessarily and adds extraneous variables to the measurements of thinking in this context.

*The films and tapes used in this study are available from the following sources:*

*Genocide. The Simon Wiesenthal Center, 9760 W. Pico Blvd, Yeshiva University, Los Angeles, Ca 90035.*

*The Bomb Factories (ABC News Closeup Special). ABC Distribution Company. Capital Cities/ABC Video Enterprises, 825 7th Avenue, New York, NY 10019-6001.*

# *Appendix A*

## SCORING RATIONALE FOR LEVELS OF THINKING

Scoring is a matter of determining the level of thinking represented in the student's paper. These Levels of Thinking are listed below, and each level is described more fully later in the manual.

Level 1: Unilateral descriptions
Level 2: Simplistic alternatives
Level 3: Emergent complexity
Level 4: Broad interpretations
Level 5: Integrated analysis

The scoring rationale for the levels of thinking emerges from a conception of thinking as a process of making meanings. At least three cognitive processes appear to operate when individuals confront a situation that is open to a variety of interpretations. These three processes are referred to as "strands" that help define the five levels of thinking. Each of these strands is discussed below.

### *Strands*

Individuals encountering a complex situation employ at least three recognizable cognitive operations in making meaning of the situation. These processes are used in making the situation intelligible and in developing evaluative positions. These processes are as follows:

1. Perception and definition of the situation.
2. Imposition of an organizing structure.
3. Analysis, support, and elaboration of a position.

These processes are used at all levels of thinking. At lower levels of thinking, these processes tend to be simplistic and limited. At higher levels of thinking, these processes exhibit complexity and open possibilities for unique interpretations. These three processes are seen as strands that cut across the various levels of thinking. These strands are continua that reflect simplistic cognitive processes at one end and complex cognitive processes at the other. Thus, the level of performance on each of these strands defines the level of thinking employed in constructing an interpretation of the problem situation.

Because the strands help define the Levels of Thinking, each is defined in some detail below.

### Perception and Definition of the Situation

This strand describes the way the student represents or encodes the situation. Rarely is all of the information used. The student perceives and selects salient features to characterize the situation and give it meaning. The student's initial perceptions define the complexity seen in the issues presented. The representation of the problem sets the limits and opens the possibilities for further elaboration and analysis.

At the lower end of the strand, the student simplifies the situation and ignores information. At the upper end of the strand, the student preserves the complexity in the situation and incorporates divergent information.

### Imposition of Organizing Structure

This strand describes the construction of an organizing structure imposed on the situation that helps make sense of the situation and provides a basis for interpretation and arguments. The interpretations of the situation are constructed around certain organizing ideas or nodes. The organizing ideas may be relatively narrow and fact-like or broader and more inclusive. Additionally, this structure includes a frame of reference within which the events are interpreted. This frame of reference reflects the student's values, concerns, and world knowledge. Imposing a simple structure (few nodes, narrow concepts, conventional framework) leads to superficial and obvious interpretations. Imposing a complex structure (many nodes, broad concepts, interpretive framework) leads to deeper analysis and integrated, comprehensive interpretations.

At the lower end of the strand, the student accepts and simplifies the framework explicitly provided. The interpretation employs narrowly defined concepts and few nodes. The student adds no new ideas or perspectives. At the upper end, the student extends the framework, bringing in world knowledge and value positions not implied by the situation. The interpretation is built around broad concepts that facilitate reorganizing, restructuring, and reconceptualizing the problem situation.

### Analysis, Support, and Elaboration

This strand describes the way the student analyzes the situation and supports a position. The progression from low to high is marked by a shift from descriptions to explanations. Describing is characterized by restatements of the information provided, coupled with assertions rather than reasons. Explaining is characterized by an integrated network of relationships supporting a particular approach to the problem.

At the lower end of the strand, the student paraphrases information and uses assertions, simple rules, and appeals to authority. At the upper end, the student constructs networks of casual relationships, applies principles, uses analogies, generalizes, and extrapolates.

### *Strands as Interactive Processes*

These mental operations are defined as separate processes for analysis only. These processes will interact in reciprocal ways as students perceive, structure, and elaborate the problem situation. Still, each of these three operations can be seen as strands that run through the thinking processes. These cognitive processes will be exercised in ways that lead to simplistic and shallow interpretations or to interpretations that preserve complexity and offer multifaceted solutions. These strands help define the five levels of cognitive processing discussed next.

## LEVELS OF COGNITIVE COMPLEXITY

### *Level 1: Simplistic Descriptions*

The student: Simplifies the situation. Focuses on a single idea or argument. Does not identify alternatives. Brings in no new information, meaning, or perspectives. Makes good/bad and either/or assertions. Appeals to authority or simple rules, for example, "The government should take care of its people." Simply paraphrases, restates or repeats information.

**Holocaust:**

> I think that the Holocaust could have been avoided if Hitler didn't want to start it in the first place. Hitler has never given the Jews a fair chance. He just kicked them out of their houses, separated their families, and put them in concentration camps. These Jews did not have a fair chance at life, because of Hitler.

This response to The Holocaust represents a unilateral perception of Hilter as the bad guy. The student recapitulates information given, performs no causal analysis, and simplifies the causes of the Holocaust.

**Bomb Factories:**

> I think that the government has done a lousy job in the handling of these factories. The bomb-factories are all outdated without modern improvements. There have been several accidents and health hazards but yet nothing is done. No improvements are attempted and whenever the subject is brought up it is swept under the rug. Hiding the facts is only going to make the situation worse and endanger more lives. The government doesn't even bother to make a public announcement that they have made a mistake or that there is a problem.

In the above example, there is essentially a single idea, the government has done a poor job of handling the bomb factories. No alternatives are mentioned and no new information is brought in. The supporting statements repeat or paraphrase the information given in the material.

### *Level 2: Simplistic Alternatives*

The student: Identifies simple and obvious conflicts or dilemmas, but does not pursue or analyze the conflicts. Develops a position by dismissing or ignoring one alternative and supporting the other with assertions and simple explanations rather than through deeper assessment of the situation.

**Holocaust:**

> I think the slayings of the Jews was probably close to one of the meanest things in history. I really don't think it was necessary because the Jews knew where they stood, they were degraded enough by having to wear the patches. Hitler wanted a master race, he had it, none of the Jews could have done anything about the discrimination. They could have tried to

> revolt but they would have been slaughtered by the German army. I guess Hitler did it just to prove his power to the rest of the world.

In this interpretation of the Holocaust, the student apparently tries to understand more fully both the German position and the Jewish response. Although the analysis remains at a shallow level, perplexity is expressed about the German actions in view of their apparent accomplishment of the goals. There is a minimal attempt at cause-and-effect analysis in considering the alternatives open to the Jews.

**Bomb Factories**:

> What they are doing should be stopped right away. I mean, how many bombs do we need, if only one can destroy the world? The people are getting unfair treatment because their whole family is getting exposed to it. The company needs to admit to making the mistake and correct it. It's not fair for us. They are making bombs to kill other people (enemies), but while they're making them, they're killing us. They need to get a solution to this problem, so that no one will be in danger! It was also very irresponsible of one of the DOE employees to give his approval, when he didn't even go into the factory in the first place. Something needs to be done because I don't want to be put in that kind of danger here in Indiana.

In the Bomb Factories example, the student introduces the dilemma of the government's killing people while also trying to protect them. The student also introduces the idea that one bomb can destroy the entire world, so further production seems unnecessary. However, the main focus is on the unfairness of this situation to the people near the plant and the population in general. Simplistic and obvious solutions are offered such as: "Something needs to be done..," " What they are doing should be stopped," and "They need to get a solution to this problem." These suggestions are not elaborated or further analyzed.

### *Level 3: Emergent Complexity*

The student: Identifies more than one possible explanation or perspective. Establishes and preserves complexity. Introduces new elements. Supports position through comparisons and simple causal statements.

**Holocaust:**

> The crimes committed by Hitler and the Nazi organization are unforgettable and unforgivable. It has been more than forty years but the memory of the people who died under the hate of Hitler will live on. It is almost unconceivable how no group took a stand against Hitler's actions. It is pretty obvious what happened throughout Germany. What is the excuse of America? Understandably the Germans were happy with Hitler's leadership. Called the supreme race, they were faced with helping the Nazis or death, but this does not explain why so many believe Hitler, why so many took his word as law. Nazi Germany put up a facade to hide the evil machine of terror running the death camps. This prevented the Jews from witnessing their own fate, but this awful crime could have been prevented if some power like America would have questioned the Germans about their "camps."I see no reason why the Holocaust should have progressed or even started in the first place. Somebody could and should have done something to prevent this from happening.

The student is trying to examine one complex idea about the Holocaust. Mainly, the focus is on why someone didn't stop this from happening. Examined are the German, Jewish, and American views. Many pertinent ideas to the argument are left out. This is evident in the discussion of why America didn't get involved. Within this argument, the student seems to take a black and white sort of outlook. The complexity behind getting involved is absent and the assertion that "this awful crime could have been prevented if some power like America" got involved only further simplifies the situation. There do, however, appear to be reasonable connections concerning the Germans' involvement.

**Bomb Factories:**

> I feel sorrow for our country, the people who live in the area, people who work in the factories, and the government officials and office holders in the plants. My sorrow for the country begins with the destruction of our own people for the sake of power. If we have to stoop so low as to kill ourselves over something that has been so over produced, what else will they do? The down winders are so light hearted about it all, it seems. They seem to just want back what was taken away from them. Their life. What seems so incredible is, how they just want them to keep waste away and not want them to stop production all together. Why? because they see they can't just stop all at once and leave so many jobless. I realize they depend greatly on their pay, so would I. Government officials who have such a burden on their shoulders, must be wondering. Are we doing the right thing? National Security, or a few cancerous farmers, and waste for miles. I realize it must be hard, but why lie? Can't they face what they've done? Probably not, neither could I. I can't stand what they've done.

In this example, complexity is preserved by identifying conflicting perspectives: national security versus health and safety, short-term solutions (keep waste away) versus long term solutions (stop production), and stopping production versus maintaining jobs. Even the obvious need to tell the truth is made complicated by the internal conflicts of the government officials.

### *Level 4: Broad Interpretations*

The student: Uses broad ideas to help define and interpret the situation. Manipulates ideas within the perspective established. Has a clearly recognizable explanatory theme. Integrates ideas into subassemblies, each supporting a component of the explanation.

**Holocaust:**

> The Holocaust was the manifestation of a people's frustrations and fear. After WWI, Germany was humiliated and destroyed economically. Jews, who had no homeland of their own were looked at as "parasites". The Jews were often middle to upper class citizens. When the Germans suffered they saw the jewish people doing well, they blamed the Jews. When there is a time of pain and frustration people looked for scapegoats. They do this because they feel inadequate about themselves. A lack of confidence one might say. It is much easier to blame another for your own misfortunes than yourself. When a person makes a mistake, and is confident of himself, he doesn't go out an look for someone to blame it on, no, that person will continue working on a solution to the problem because he has the confidence in himself that he will find it. The Holocaust happened because the German people lost their self-confidence from WWI and had to look elsewhere. The Jewish extermination was the solution.

The first sentence of this essay serves as an advanced organizer. The theme is laid out and then unfolded step-by-step. Although the organization stems from one dimension of the Holocaust, the student has stated and developed a well integrated overview of the situation.The essay communicates the position we see taken in the film and could serve as an excellent summary of what is depicted.

**Bomb Factories:**

> America's bomb factories are obviously a national disgrace. What it all boils down to, is that the government has decided that in order for our country to have a strong national defense, efficiency must be valued over the security and lives of certain individuals. The obvious answer to the problem is to increase the safety of the bomb factories, but in fact, it isn't as simple as that. In the first place, the factories are so old and outdated, that it would take more than a simple repair job to make them safe, and this of course, costs money. Secondly, and

> probably one of our government's worst fears, is that in order to modernize the plants, they would have to be shut down, which would give Russia an advantage over us in the quantity of arms production. Thirdly, an interesting viewpoint that is held by many people, is that the government is purposefully bloating the scandal out of proportion, in order to get a more modern and efficient means of weapon production. Thus, we see that reform in this case is a rather sticky situation. What it all boils down to is a question of values.
>
> Does the government value the lives of the few, or the "security" of the many. In this issue, there are no absolutes. Certainly, it is inhumane to kill off these people, but are their lives valuable enough to jeopardize the security of the nation? or is security really in jeopardy?

In the example above, the student presents the conflict of efficient production versus the lives of individuals. He points out that increasing the safety of the factories is an obvious solution, but the solution is complicated by the age of the factories and the time required for the production of the bombs. Additionally, the government may be manipulating public concern about safety. Each of the established components brings in new information not presented in the materials. The student's explanatory theme is clearly a reference to values as a basis for decisions.

### *Level 5: Integrated Analysis*

The student: Restructures or reconceptualizes the situation and approaches the problem from a new point of view. Constructs a network of cause-and-effect relationships. Integrates and extrapolates ideas. Arrives at new interpretations by analogy, application of principles, generalizations, and utilization of world knowledge. Constructs an organizing framework, sketches connections, and predicts consequences.

**Holocaust:**

> I think the Holocaust was a very terrible event. It is very hard to imagine the magnitude of six million people being killed and what today would be like if it hadn't of happened. I don't think we can blame German soldiers and citizens for hating the Jews, because they were taught to hate them their entire lives. For our entire lives, we've been told that the Russians are the evil people and I'm sure that many of our soldiers would have no problem killing innocent Russians. It is just a tragedy that governments have the power to abuse the education system to bias citizens against other races, religions, or ideologies.
>
> I am surprised we didn't learn a lesson from the Holocaust. America had a chance to speak out and to try to help the Jews during WWII, but we didn't care. It is apparent to me that we still don't care, because we allow white South Africans to illegally arrest and torture black South Africans, and we allow the Middle East to be a place of constant warfare among people who hate each other's ethnic background. It has taken a tremendous outcry from Russian dissidents about their lack of civil rights to get us to at least pressure Russia into improving the situation. I wonder what it will take to make people care about all of the atrocities in the world.

The student conceptualizes the situation within a framework that considers political influences that shape societal values. A new interpretation of the situation is arrived at by an analogy between the way Germans were taught to think about Jews and how we are taught to think about Russians. The student constructs this view by utilizing broad concepts of government-controlled education and propaganda to explain the emergence of hate and prejudice on a national scale. In the second paragraph, the student elaborates the theme of American indifference to human rights violations. The student draws parallels between our former lack of involvement and our current indifference to the atrocities of the world.

**Bomb Factories:**

After seeing this videotape and reading the article it is obvious America has a problem disposing of its nuclear waste. Although just two plants were mentioned, I'm sure that nearly every nuclear plant in the country is in someway illegally disposing of nuclear waste. I think this is a great injustice to Americans, especially today when so many Americans are concentrating on their health. In the every day hustle and bustle Americans can be inconsiderate and uncaring, but when major issues come up I think Americans form strong opinions and are willing to unite together. This is such a case where Americans are realizing that we don't need as many warheads anymore and that production must slow down. We must concentrate our efforts, time and money, on finding out how to safely dispose of nuclear waste, and all other industrial waste, and how to safely disarm and store nuclear weapons.

Nuclear energy has only been used for forty or fifty years. I consider us to still be in the early stages of nuclear energy where we can't realize the full potential and dangers of nuclear energy. American industry boomed in the late 1800's and was a heavy polluter. Now after 100 years of heavy industry we are clamping down on pollution with our knowledge of industry. I hope that we can learn from the past and put restraint on our nuclear energy industry now instead of 50 more years from now.

Most importantly I think we must immediately begin extensive research on how to safely control the nuclear waste that is so quickly created.

The most notable aspect of this response is the construction of a global organizing framework. An almost sociological view of Americans is presented. Historical ideas are woven into an integrated frame of reference: trends in science/industry and human interventions concerning our past, present, and future lives. Ideas are well integrated and extrapolated. The bomb factories are viewed as one instance of the more general problem of industrial pollution. Nuclear energy is perceived as a young industry for which the future potential and dangers are unknown. There is extensive use of generalizations and world knowledge.

### *Scoring Strategies*

Before scoring student essays, it is advisable to first read through a sample of the essays to get a holistic impression of the range and variety of responses. The papers might be tentatively sorted into levels consistent with the scoring criteria. One should not expect that essays will be found that fit each level. For example, Level 5 is very difficult to achieve. The scoring criteria should not be adjusted to fit a particular local group.

After the initial evaluation, the essays can be analyzed in greater detail, matching the student's work against the criteria presented for each level and comparing the work with the examples.

During the analysis, it is helpful to focus on how the situation is perceived. For instance, in a Level 1 response the problem is taken as given or it is overly simplified. The student will open, progress, and close on the same note. Each statement seems to reiterate the initial simplistic view and does not go further. At Levels 2 and 3, the student may open with a simplistic statement but will gradually transform this statement into broader, more open-ended ideas and dilemmas. At the higher levels new perspectives are established and patterns of greater complexity are seen in the situation.

It is also helpful to examine the structure that emerges as the student copes with the material and interprets the situation. The structure is defined by the breadth of concepts, number of nodes, and the nature of the interpretive framework.

At Level 1, interpretations are built around a single idea leading to black/white, good/bad positions. At Levels 2 and 3, several viewpoints are considered that serve as the points around which the interpretations are organized. At Levels 4 and 5, broad concepts, world knowledge, and organizing frameworks or themes lead to more multifaceted and better integrated interpretations.

Last, it is helpful to examine the quality and complexity of the analysis and support. From Level 1 to Level 5, there is a transition from description to explanation and analysis. At levels 1 and 2, the response appears mostly as a description of the situation. At Level 3, the student begins explaining how parts of the situation are interconnected. By Levels 4 and 5, the response is noticeably analytic. The analysis is accomplished through use of cause-and-effect relationships and increased connections between ideas. World knowledge is employed to broaden the perspective and add new dimensions to the analysis.

Obviously, the cognitive processes we have described will not be equally evident in all essays. The scorer will have to make best estimates of the level of thinking represented. As experience is obtained in using this rationale, scoring will become increasingly easy. Until this point is reached, constant reference to the scoring guide and the examples will be the best assurance for reliable scoring.

# *Appendix B*

## PRACTICE EXAMPLES

Below are 10 practice examples of actual student responses, 5 from The Holocaust and 5 from The Bomb Factories. The essays are not corrected for punctuation. Our scoring and a discussion of the rationale for placement on a specific level follows the example. You should make notes on each example of your own rationale for why that example should be placed at a particular level and then compare those notes with the rationale discussed in the answer section.

### *The Holocaust*

1. I don't understand why people discriminate against other people. So what if they have a different religion, that doesn't mean we can kill them. The Jews to the Germans were the same as blacks to us. But we didn't try to anihilate their race. Racism against the blacks is still going on today. I had no idea about how much racism was going on here. When I read about it, I was astounded. Like I said before, I just can't understand why people do this kind of thing. They are people too! Just because you don't like them doesn't give you the right to kill all of them.

2. I feel that if I could go back in time, I would speak out for the Jews to try to get them help. I would say that its wrong. I would state that I care. I would get people to back me up. I

would destroy the Germans for what they were doing. What happened then is over with, but people are still suffering today. There was absolutely no excuse for what happened. Hitler was a mad man and I am glad he killed himself. I only wish someone else would have done it sooner before the Holocaust had to happen.

**3.** I know that the Holocaust really occurred, but I don't want to believe it. I don't want to face the fact that people were made to suffer in this way or that people could be so inhumane and cruel.

I try to have faith in humanity. I believe that we should love one another. The Holocaust does more than prove my faith to be misguided. It shatters me. It horrifies me.

Six million deaths are not comprehensible. I can not feel an individual grief for each victim. I feel a wringing sort of agony, guilt and horror which does not lessen with time as the pain of an individual loss does. Shall I paint the future blackly? I can not believe that the Holocaust can ever happen again but I can not believe it ever happened. Have people really changed. Have we all learned a lesson against death? I live in the era of the "winnable nuclear war". I can't be sure that another group of fanatics mightn't victimize innocent people again.

Actually, I don't feel particularly worse that the victims were Jews than if they weren't. Being a Jew is not an important part of my identity.

This doesn't lessen the pain and grief a bit, of course. People are my one and only ethnic group when it comes down to it, so yes I'm outraged at what they've done, what they've had done to them.

It would have been terrible to be a Jew in 1939, but what would it have been like to be a Nazi? The villains of the Holocaust are few, the rest were honestly devoted.

Yet! They should have had conscience against such slaughter. Don't people have an innate sense of compassion? They must.

Prejudice is a twister. Prejudice is always always a lie. Prejudice denies free will.

"Let it never happen again!!" I am so vehement. But I wonder. What is happening in Africa, in Turkey, in Nicaragua, in New York City right now?

A Holocaust doesn't need concentration camps or "showers." Just prejudice and anger. Just weapons and flesh and blood. Just the ignorance of the apathetic world. And the world is so apathetic. Don't people have an innate sense of compassion? They must. They must.

**4.** I personally feel that the whole situation was cruel and unjustified. The thought of the Holocaust scares me, especially when people say it could happen again. Although I don't think it ever could. WWII serves as a very harsh lesson to the nations of the world and there were programs (UN, CIA, etc.) and agencies set up after the war to prevent this from happening. (Another reason I don't think this could ever happen again is because discrimination isn't that strong a feeling in a particularly powerful nation.) It always shocks me to think that one man with the right conditions in a country could cause such a strong movement towards innocent people. I feel sorry for the followers of the Jewish religion because of what their people went through. I don't feel there is anything that could ever make up for lost relatives and the cruelty. It is a situation that I will never forget happened and I don't think the world will either.

**5.** The Holocaust was a very hard lesson that the world had to experience. I do not think that all this killing and murdering of a mass of people simply because of their religion had to take place. It could have been partially avoided if the rest of the world had more sense than simply not getting involved. This terrifying event could have ended in a much less fierce way.

I am Jewish and my family knows a few survivors from the Ghettos. I know that I am, and will always be, a part of the Jewish race. I will have fear of another Holocaust inside me for as long as I live, but I hope that the people on earth have learned the lesson and will not let another Holocaust take place.

Although it was a terrifying experience, I do think that in a way the anger and the hopelessness of a people during the depression had to come out somehow. If it did not come out on the Jews, it would have came out on the Blacks, Catholics, Buddhists, or any other members of a specific race or religion.

**The Bomb Factories**

1. It sounds like the government and factory personnel have been covering up something they've known for a long time. Of course its not right, but the wrong can not be undone. They can correct the conditions & maybe give the people, that have suffered because of them, compensations.

If the government does deny responsibility it will be like the guy said "...you don't have a republic." Isn't a republic what the U.S. is proud of. If people can't count on their own government to stay straight with them, then who can anyone trust?

I feel sorry for the workers of the plants that didn't know about this who may be getting the blame. In the production line there are so many people that do little jobs, I'm sure there has to be one or two that didn't know. Like I said before we can't undo anything but the people deserve to be told the truth at the very least & maybe compensation.

2. The government is really stuck in a position it is hard to get out of. They should have started 10 years ago. This may be just a political ploy to get the U.S. citizens in the mood for spending billions on the factories, after all there are not mass numbers of people dying. The Executives and Engineers work in the factory too and they are the people supposedly pushing production. I think it does hurt the environment But so does all industry. They could make it a bit better for the workers

and surrounding residents but there is risk involved in everything.

3. The problem of contamination by radioactive material has been around for a long time, but only now are we beginning to pay attention to it. Only now, after innocent people have suffered the effects of exposure to radioactive materials, do we even recognize this problem. It seems a shame that these people had to suffer before anyone would listen. We should have thought about this a long time ago. The people who design the bomb factories supposedly are experts, and as experts in their field, should be well aware that exposure to radioactive materials is damaging to people. I suspect they did know the dangers - but did they sit down and think of a way to avoid them? The consequences and effects of setting up a bomb factory should have been carefully considered before the plant was even opened. Perhaps, with some advanced planning, we could have avoided the problem by finding solutions to the potential problem first, before it became a problem. As it was, there was either no thought given to future consequences, or, if plans were made on how to deal with radioactive waste generated by the plant, these plans were often not carried out completely. I don't know if this was because it was purely an oversight, or if it was that safety considerations were knowingly abandoned in the name of faster or more efficient production. The reason why this problem exists is not the issue, though. The issue, the thing we must focus on now, is to try to find a way to help the people who have suffered from exposure and to make sure it doesn't happen again. We need to solve this problem now, quickly, so no more innocent lives are touched by suffering from exposure to radioactive wastes from these bomb factories. We owe the people in the world their safety, after all these bombs are supposed to protect us by providing national security, when in reality they are hurting us by contaminating people with exposure to dangerous materials.

4. I think that those families have the right to complain about the bomb factories, because I also think that from the bomb factories that is how all those people got cancer and that's not right.

It's not a good thing to have around if it's killing people. They need to be more careful and aware of what they're doing. And they should do something about radioactive-iodine releases from weapons plants, so it won't be giving thyroid problems.

5. With regard to the problem of the bomb factories, I think we have to make some decisions as to where we stand. We must decide how we feel about bomb production in general. If bomb production is not necessary, why not just shut down the factories? On the other hand, we may need to produce nuclear weapons. In that case, we must decide if producing bombs is more important than screwing up the lives of the innocent people who are being contaminated. Also, we must realize we are destroying our environment. If bomb production absolutely must continue, then we must examine ways to reduce, rather than eliminate, contamination. We could, for instance, use only one factory, and put in an isolated area where harm to people and the environment would be minimalized.

In my opinion bomb production is quite unnecessary in the first place, so there is no need for the factories. Without the factories, there would be no contamination, and we could spend our time, money, and energies pursuing something besides the production of nuclear weapons.

### *Discussions of The Holocaust Practice Exercises*

1. (Level 2): The student starts out with an analogy between Jews and blacks but does not go on to analyze this relationship or bring up any other points about discrimination or how this situation could have occurred. Instead, the student only reveals that the situation is not understood and makes no

attempt to think through it. The ideas expressed are simply statements and not explanations. This appears to be a step above Level 1 because the student is not simply paraphrasing or describing and does introduce some openness.

2. (Level 1): This example contains no analysis. The essay is full of assertions and feeling but no explanations are attempted. The view taken is a good-guy/bad-guy theory of history.

3. (Level 5): This response is marked by expressions of feeling and an engaging style. Scoring becomes a matter of disembedding the analytic framework and tracking the cognitive processes. For this student, the Holocaust raises questions about the nature of humanity and whether humanity has changed since the time of the Holocaust. In seeking answers, the student notes that we live in a era of the "winnable nuclear war." The student maintains a broad perspective in identifying herself and avoids the simplification of seeing the Nazis as villains. With the Nazis though, compassion is absent, prejudice distorts, and current examples suggest that the problems continue in an apathetic world. This response reveals an integrated analysis that starts and ends on the nature of humanity. The causes of the Holocaust are seen in the human phenomena of prejudice, anger, ignorance, and apathy. Unresolved is the role of compassion as a countervailing force.

4. (Level 3): This response notes that such organizations as the UN and the CIA might help prevent a future Holocaust. Two additional ideas are advanced: powerful nations have less need to discriminate, and "one man and the right conditions in a country" could cause such a movement. These ideas illustrate causal thinking, but there is no further development.

5. (Level 4): Three aspects or views of the problem are discussed: avoiding or lessening the problem, learning a lesson from the Holocaust, and the hopelessness during the depression as a causal factor. A new perspective is introduced

in examining how the conditions of the times elicited prejudice and the resulting crimes against a race of people. The student goes on to generalize how the same type of prejudice could have been inflicted on another race or religious group. Overall, this is a high Level 4 because of the broad perceptions and the beginning of a more global frame of reference. However, the essay is not fully integrated and the student does not fully elaborate and support the basic premise that this may have had to happen but could have been less severe.

### *Discussions of The Bomb Factories Practice Exercises*

1. (Level 2): The response focuses on more than one aspect of the situation. The student expresses concern about correcting conditions and compensating victims, but the major concern is the responsibility of the government. An alternative is not explicitly stated then eliminated, but government responsibility is linked to the broader concept of "a republic."

2. Level 3): The opening sentence communicates a perception of the problem as difficult and complex. The student brings in new viewpoints: solutions should have started much earlier, and there is a possibility that current concern is simply a ploy to spend more on the plants. There is limited support for these two propositions. This response is placed at Level 3, since the student clearly approaches the problem from a point of view not present in the materials. Some support is provided for the viewpoints, but the analysis is not developed.

3. (Level 5): In this example a time perspective is established within which the problem is viewed. Within this perspective the problem is conceptualized as one of poor planning. This theme is developed by pointing to the role of experts, considering the consequences of opening bomb factories, and

probing the reasons that concerns for safety were abandoned. The construction of an organizing frame of reference was the major consideration in assigning this response to Level 5. The author goes on to note that the background reasons are not the current issue and broadens the problem to include the safety of the "people in the world."

4. (Level 1): Both the issue and the solution are a simplification of the problem: "It's not a good thing to have around if its killing people" and "They need to be more careful." Assertions are supported with more assertions.

5. (Level 4): The student introduces and reasons from an explanatory theme: "how we feel about bomb production in general." Broad concerns are discussed including the necessity of bombs, environmental concerns, and possible solutions. These components are integrated into the explanatory theme.

## TEST EXAMPLES

Below are 10 test examples. After these examples the authors' rating is given. You should use these examples for interrater reliability.

1. **Bomb Factories:** Since life comes before anything else it is only human nature to protect it. The reasoning behind why there are weapons and why they are being produced is simple, it is for national defense of the U.S. to protect the lives of American citizens; but there is no justification for building nuclear plants or not shutting down nuclear plants after the harm of these plants has been recognized. The U.S. government's reason for building nuclear plants is to protect the citizens of the U.S., not harm them. I am shown that in this day and age with distrust between countries, weapons are necessary, but having enough weapons to destroy the Earth three times is just ridiculous. Therefore I must say

that building nuclear weapons is not justified. Before the time of nuclear weapons wars were limited to the countries and the generation that the war occurs in, but now not only will it destroy a generation, but as we have seen in Japan, it will harm the next. The U.S. made a big deal about the Chernobyl plant, well it should turn around and take a look at our own plants. After all, nuclear weapons were made to protect the U.S. not destroy it.

2. **Bomb Factories:** I think it is really sad that these people, for one thing, stay there! I would move so I wouldn't stay there. If there has been more than one case of people getting cancer then why stay there. Something should be done about the places that are making the weapons. They are supposed to be making them to defend us not to kill us!! I really think that they shouldn't be made in the first place then everybody will be safe. As for Zinser, I think he should sue them for his two boys cancer!! They have to go through a lot of pain and so does he and its only fair for the people at this plant to feel it too.

3. **Holocaust:** I think the Holocaust was a horrible experience for most everyone involved. The number of Jews killed is absolutely disgusting and should have attempted to be stopped by American forces. I did not realize the full extent of the Holocaust until I heard the number of people killed and the stories from this tape. Some of the stories about the Jewish people being forced into the Ghettos and then into the gas chambers were frightening when I think about what it would have been like if I was Jewish and lived at that time. I also have a hard time understanding how a whole nation can turn against one section of people in such a violent manner without someone speaking up for the people being hurt. This seems ridiculous to me, of course I am living in the United States and have an easy life, as a citizen, compared to a lot of citizens in other countries.

4. **Holocaust:** Details of the Holocaust read almost like a terrible science fiction novel, the brutality is beyond belief. This situation is an extreme case of persecution of a minority gone wild. Hopefully, the Holocaust will be vividly remembered far into the future as a warning of what extreme situations of desperation can do. The Holocaust must be the nightmare, not just of Jews, but of any minority who might be enslaved, imprisoned or killed because the majority has turned against them. It is unbelievable that poverty and a ruined economy can create such desperation, and irrational anger in normally sane people. Thus it is vital to protect all individual freedoms and try to maintain economic and political stability to prevent another future outbreak of such terror and violence.

5. **Bomb Factories:** I think it is ridiculous that factories are doing so much damage and nothing is being done about it. Sure the factories make bombs, which will be used to kill the enemy. What they are doing isn't just killing the enemy, but their own people. They are letting all of this bad material into the atmosphere, which is causing a lot of people to get cancer. It seems to me that the people running these factories don't care about anything but making bombs. They must have demented minds. I don't know how anyone could want to make bombs. In a sense they are murderers. They kill the people around the factories and when they set the bomb off, it will kill millions of people. I'm sorry, I really don't see why we need to make bombs. God created us and he should be the one to destroy us, not ourselves.

6. **Bomb Factories:** Through the tape and magazine articles many problems were mentioned. I feel that America needs to work with these problems. Why I feel this way is because it has killed and endangered many lives. I know that the United States thinks that having weapons are important, but in the process of making these weapons they are killing their own people.

I think that the U. S. is responsible for their citizens and should try to reconstruct new factories which are safe. They need to somehow destroy the old factories and dispose of all radioactive materials, etc. in a safe way. That safe way is what America needs to find. We need scientists to research this. I think that the money we would use to clean up and make safety features would be worth the lives they can save.

7. **Holocaust:** I think that the Holocaust was sick. I do not see how anyone could take the life of another just because he had different beliefs. Americans or someone else should have stepped in and done something to help the Jews rather than allowing Hitler to slaughter them. If the Americans would have done something, they could have saved the lives of some of the Jews. Everyone is responsible for letting this happen. People can not just blame the slaughter of the Jews on Germany, because the United States just sat back and watched it happen.

8. **Holocaust:** The Jews had no right to be treated the way they were. The Nazis only saw things in their point of view and didn't put themselves in the places of the Jews. The Nazis really didn't know how painful it was and how disgusting it was. The Nazis should now get their turn and see what it was like. If such human beings could kill others, then they don't deserve to live themselves. Torture of that kind should not be allowed no matter who it is towards. The Nazis had no right to treat the Jews that way. The Nazis should now have to pay the consequences.

9. **Bomb Factories:** The government is really stuck in a position it is hard to get out of. They should have started 10 years ago. This may be just a political ploy to get the U.S. citizens in the mood for spending billions on the factories, after all there are not mass numbers of people dying. The Executives & Engineers work in the factory too and they are the people supposedly pushing production. I think it does

hurt the environment. But so does all industry. They could make it a bit better for the workers & surrounding residents but there is risk involved in everything. This is also boring cuz I've seen it before!

10. **Holocaust:** The first thing that comes to mind when referring to the Holocaust is disgust. I fail to see where one man's obsession should result in the persecution of over 6 million people. Germany had been humiliated by the Treaty of Versailles and sought revenge in any way they could. Instead of blaming themselves for their downfall, the Jews became a scapegoat. They were seen as an inferior race, just as the white Americans viewed the blacks. Unlike the discrimination in the U.S., this was a lot more severe. It is still not and won't ever be logical that the Nazi's found it necessary to take so many innocent lives. The Jewish people had never done any harm to them except being themselves. Many times I use ignorance as a reason for prejudice but in that case there seems to be no reasonable explanation. It is an example of what kind of things can occur in this world and how many people think. I strongly resent and disagree with the old system of slavery and I see this as a worse treatment of human beings. People should be allowed to "live and let live" and not kill.

Answers to Test Examples

1. Level 5
2. Level 1
3. Level 3
4. Level 5
5. Level 2
6. Level 4
7. Level 2
8. Level 1
9. Level 3
10. Level 4

# *Appendix C*

## Answer Sheet for The Bomb Factories

You have just seen a tape and read a magazine article about the bomb factories. Tell us what you think about this situation. Take a few minutes to reflect on what you have heard and seen. Take your time. Describe and explain your thoughts as completely and fully as possible.

## REFERENCES


Armstrong, P., & McDaniel, E. (1987, June). *Approaches to the measurement of thinking processes.* Paper presented at The Third National Conference on Thinking, Cincinnati, OH.

Bartlett, F. (1958). *Thinking: An experimental and social study.* New York, NY: Basic Books.

Bruner, J. (1986). *Actual minds, possible worlds.* Cambridge, MA: Harvard University Press.

Cacioppo, J. T., & Petty, R. E. (1982). The need for cognition. *Journal of Personality & Social Psychology*, 42, 116-131.

*California Achievement Test* (1985). Monterey, CA: McGraw Hill.

Cox, B. E. (1987). Cohesion and content organization in the narrative and expository writing of children. (Unpublished doctoral dissertation, Northwestern University, 1986). *Dissertation Abstracts International*, (University Microfilm No. DAO 58785).

Ennis, R. H., & Weir, E. (1985). *The Ennis-Weir critical thinking essay test.* Pacific Grove, CA: Midwest Publications.

Ennis, R. H., Millman, J., & Tomko, T. N. (1985). *Cornell critical thinking tests: Level X & level Z manual*, 3rd edition. Pacific Grove, CA: Midwest Publications.

Galotti, K. M. (1989). Approaches to studying formal and everyday reasoning. *Psychological Bulletin*, 105 (3), 331-351.

Halliday, M. A. K. (1985). *An introduction to functional grammar.* Baltimore, MD: Edward Arnold.

Harvey, O. J., Hunt, D. E., & Schroder, H. M. (1961). *Conceptual systems and personality organization.* New York: John Wiley & Sons.

Helmstadter, G. C. (1985). Review of Watson-Glaser critical thinking appraisal. *The Ninth Mental Measurement Yearbook, Vol II.* Buros Institute of Mental Measurement, University of Nebraska Press.

James, William. (1979). Great men and their environment. In F. H. Burkhardt, F. Bowers, & I. K. Skrupskelis (Eds.). *The works of William James: The will to believe.* Cambridge, Harvard University Press. (Reprinted from *Atlantic Monthly,* October, 1880)

Langer, J. (1986). *Children reading and writing: Structures and strategies.* Norwood, NJ: Ablex.

Lawrence, C. L. & Stewart, R. (1990, April). Cognitive complexity and discourse structure in adolescent's writing. In Carl Bereiter (Chair), *Expertise and the acquisition of literacy skills.* Symposium conducted at the annual meeting of the American Educational Research Association, Boston.

McDaniel, E., & Ferreyra, Y. (1989). *The learning behaviors checklist: An instrument to measure student autonomy.* Unpublished manuscript.

McDaniel, E., & Thompson, T. (1989, June). *The Holocaust: A prototype exercise to measure thinking.* Paper presented at the Fifth National Conference on Thinking, Cincinnati, OH.

Messick, S. (1984). The nature of cognitive styles: Problems and promise in educational practice. *Educational Psychologist, 19* (2), 59-74.

Nicholls, J. G. (1989). *The competitive ethos and democratic education.* Cambridge: Harvard University Press.

Peel, E. A. (1971). *The nature of adolescent judgement.* New York, NY: Wiley-Interscience.

Peirce, C. S. (1956). The criterion of validity of reasoning. In J. Buchler (Ed.). *The philosophy of Peirce: Selected writings.* London, Routledge &

Kegan Paul (Reprinted from Lectures on Pragmatism, Harvard University, 1903).

Perkins, D. N. (1982). *Difficulties in everyday reasoning and their change with education.* Report to the Spencer Foundation. Cambridge, MA: Harvard University.

Perry, W. G. (1970). *Forms of intellectual and ethical development in the college years: A scheme.* New York, NY: Holt, Rinehart and Winston.

Rhys, W. T. (1964). *The development of logical thought in the adolescent with reference to the teaching of geography in the secondary school.* Unpublished M.Ed. Research, Birmingham University.

Rudman, H. C. (1985). Review of Ennis-Weir argumentation test, level X. *The Ninth Mental Measurement Yearbook, Vol II.* Buros Institute of Mental Measurement, University of Nebraska Press.

Schmeck, R. R., Ribich, F. D., & Ramanaiah, N. (1977). Development of a self report inventory for assessing individual differences in learning processes. *Applied Psychological Measurement, 1*, 413-431.

Schroder, H. M., Driver, M.J., & Streufert, S. (1967). *Human information processing: Individuals and groups functioning in complex social situations.* New York, NY: Holt, Rinehart and Winston.

Shiang, C. P., & McDaniel, E. (in press). The mystery of Pearl Harbor: A computer simulation to measure thinking processes. *Journal of Educational Computing Research.*

Siegel, H. (1988). *Educating reason: rationality, critical thinking, and education.* London: Routledge.

*Test of Cognitive Skills* (1987). Monterey, CA: CTB/McGraw Hill.

Vygotsky, L. S. (1962). *Thought and Language.* (E. Hanfmann & G. Vakar Eds./Trans.). Cambridge, MA: MIT Press.

Watson, G., & Glaser, E. M. (1980). *The Watson-Glaser critical thinking appraisal.* San Antonio, TX: The Psychological Corporation.

Wood, J., & McDaniel, E. (1990, February). *Correlating the results of a computer-based simulation with various achievement and affective variables.* Paper presented at the Eastern Educational Research Association meeting, Clearwater, FL.

## RELATED REFERENCES

Abele, A. (1985). Thinking about thinking: Causal, evaluative and finalistic cognitions about social situations. *European Journal of Social Psychology, 15*, 315-332.

Adams, M. J. (1989). Thinking skills curricula: Their promise and progress. *Educational Psychologist, 24*, 25-77.

Adams, A., Carnine, D., & Gersten, R. (1982). Instructional strategies for studying content area texts in the intermediate grades. *Reading Research Quarterly, 18*, 27-55.

Ames, G. J., & Murray, (1982). When two wrongs make a right: Provoking cognitive change by social conflict. *Developmental Psychology, 18*, 894-897.

Anderson, N. H. (1986). A cognitive theory of judgment and decision. In B. Brehmer, H. Jungermann, P. Lourens, & G. Secon (Eds.), *New directions in research on decision making* (pp. 63-108). Amsterdam: North-Holland.

Anderson, R. N., Greene, M. L., & Loewen, P. S. (1988). Relationships among teachers' and students' thinking skills, sense of efficacy, and student achievement. *Alberta Journal of Educational Research, 34*, 148-165.

Applebee, A. N. (1984). *Contexts for learning to write: Studies of secondary school instruction.* Norwood, NJ: Ablex Publishing Corp.

Arkes, H. R., & Hammond, K. R. (Eds.). (1986). *Judgment and decision making: An interdisciplinary reader.* Cambridge, MA: Cambridge University Press.

Baron, J. (1981). Reflective thinking as a goal of education. *Intelligence, 5*, 291-309.

Baron, J. (1985). *Rationality and intelligence.* New York: Cambridge University Press.

Baron, J., & Sternberg, R. J. (Eds.). (1986). *Teaching thinking skills: Theory and practice.* New York: Freeman.

Block, R. A. (1985). Education and thinking skills reconsidered. *American Psychologist, 40*, 574-575.

Brabeck, M. M. (1983). Critical thinking skills and reflective judgment development: Redefining the aims of higher education. *Journal of Applied Developmental Psychology, 4*, 23-24.

Bransford, J. D., & Stein, B. S. (1984). *The ideal problem solver: A guide for improving thinking, learning, and creativity.* New York: Freeman.

Bransford, J. D., Sherwood, R., Vye, N., & Rieser, J. (1986). Teaching thinking and problem solving: Research foundations. *American Psychologist, 41*, 1078-1089.

Carpenter, T. P., Peterson, P. L. (1988). Learning through instruction: The study of students' thinking during instruction in mathematics. Special Issue: Learning mathematics from instruction. *Educational Psychologist, 23*, 79-85.

Chance, P. (1986). *Thinking in the classroom: A survey of programs.* New York: Columbia University, Teachers College Press.

Chipman, S. F., Segal, J. W., & Glaser, R. (Eds.). (1985). *Thinking and learning skills: Vol. 2.* Research and open questions. Hillsdale, NJ: Erlbaum.

Costa, A. L. (1985). Toward a model of human intellectual functioning. In A. L. Costa (Ed.), *Developing minds: A resource for teaching thinking.* Alexandria, VA: Association for Supervision and Curriculum Development.

Covington, M. V., Crutchfield, R. S., Davies, L., & Olton, R. M. (1974). *The productive thinking program: A course in learning to think.* Columbus, OH: Merrill.

de Bono, E. (1975). *CoRT thinking.* Blandford, Dorset, England: Direct Education Services Ltd.

de Bono, E. (1976). *Teaching thinking.* London: Temple Smith.

Deci, E. L., & Ryan, R. M. (1985). *Intrinsic motivation and self-determination in human behavior.* New York: Plenum Press.

Dillon, R. F., & Sternberg, R. J. (Eds.). (1986). *Cognition and instruction.* San Diego, CA: Academic Press.

Embretson, S., Schneider, L. M., & Roth, D. L. (1986). Multiple processing strategies and the construct validity of verbal reasoning tests. *Journal of Educational Measurement, 23*, 13-32.

Ennis, R. H. (1987). A taxonomy of critical thinking dispositions and abilities. In J. B. Baron & R. J. Sternberg (Eds.), *Teaching thinking skills*. New York: Freeman.

Ennis, R. H. (1981). Rational thinking and educational practice. In J. F. Soltis (Ed.), *Philosophy of education* (80th Yearbook of the National Society for the Study of Education, Vol. 1, pp. 143-183). Chicago: National Society for the Study of Education.

Ennis, R. H. (1976). An alternative to Piaget's conceptualization of logical competence. *Child Development*, *47*, 903-913.

Ennis, R. H. (1962). A concept of critical thinking. *Harvard Educational Review*, *32*, 81-111.

Eisner, E. W. (1965). Critical thinking: Some cognitive components. *Teachers College Record*, *66*, 624-634.

Epstein, S., & Meier, P. (1989). Constructive thinking: A broad coping variable with specific components. *Journal of Personality and Social Psychology*, *57*, 332-350.

Erickson, J. R., & Jones, M. R. (1978). Thinking. *Annual Review of Psychology*, *29*, 61-91.

Feuerstein, R., Rand, Y., Hoffman, M., Hoffman, M., & Miller, R. (1980). *Instrumental enrichment*. Baltimore, MD: University Park Press.

Fontana, D., Lotwick, G., Simon, A., & Ward, L. O. (1983). A factor analysis of critical, convergent and divergent thinking tests in a group of male polytechnic students. *Personality and Individual Differences*, *4*, 687-688.

Gagn é, R. (1988). Some reflections on thinking skills. *Instructional Science*, *17*, 387-390.

Gagne', R. (1980). Learnable aspects of problem solving. *Educational Psychologist*, *15*, 84-92.

Gans, R. (1940). *Critical reading comprehension in the intermediate grades*. New York: Columbia University Teachers College.

Gaskins, I. W. (1988-89). Teachers as thinking coaches: Creating strategic learners and problem solvers. *Journal of Reading, Writing, and Learning Disabilities International*, *4*, 35-48.

Greeno, J. G. (1989). A perspective on thinking. Special Issue: Children and their development: Knowledge base, research agenda, and social policy application. *American Psychologist, 44*, 134-141.

Haan, N. (1975). Hypothetical and actual moral reasoning in a situation of civil disobedience. *Journal of Personality and Social Psychology, 32*, 255-270.

Hagert, G., Waern, Y., & Tarland, S. A. (1982). Open and closed models of understanding in conditional reasoning. *Acta Psychologica, 52*, 41-59.

Halpern, D. F. (1989). *Thought and knowledge: An introduction to critical thinking*. Hillsdale, NJ: Erlbaum.

Heiman, M., & Slomianko, J. (1986). *Critical thinking skills.* Washington, DC: National Education Association.

Henle, M. (1962). On the relation between logic and thinking. *Psychological Review, 69*, 366-378.

Hennessey, B. A., & Amabile, T. M. (1987). *Creativity and learning.* Washington, DC: National Education Association.

Herrnstein, R. J., Nickerson, R. S., de Sanchez, M., & Swets, J. A. (1986). Teaching thinking skills. *American Psychologist, 41*, 1279-1289.

Hitchcock, D. (1983). *Critical thinking: A guide to evaluating information.* Toronto, Canada: Methuen Publications.

Holland, J. H., Holyoak, K. J., Nisbett, R. E., & Thagard, P. R. (1986). *Induction: Processes of Inference, Learning, and Discovery.* Cambridge, MA: The MIT Press.

Hudgins, B. B., & Edelman, S. (1988). *Children's self-directed critical thinking.* Journal of Educational Research, 81, 262-273.

Hudgins, B. B., & Edelman, S. (1986). Teaching critical thinking skills to fourth and fifth graders through teacher-led small-group discussions. *Journal of Educational Research, 79*, 333-342.

Jones, B. F., Palincsar, A. S., Ogle, D. S., & Carr, E. G. (Eds.). (1987). *Strategic teaching and learning: Cognitive instruction in the content areas.* Alexandria, VA: Association for Supervision and Curriculum Development.

Kagan, D. M. (1988). Measurements of divergent and complex thinking. *Educational and Psychological Measurement, 48*, 873-884.

Kahane, H. (1988). *Logic and contemporary rhetoric: The use of reason in everday life* (5th ed.). Belmont, CA: Wadsworth Publishing Company.

Kamil, M. L. (1987). Can thinking be taught? *Contemporary Psychology, 32*, 548-549.

Keeley, S. M., & Browne, M. N. (1986). How college seniors operationalize critical thinking behavior. *College Student Journal, 20*, 389-395.

Kelley, D. (1988). *The art of reasoning.* New York: W. W. Norton.

King, J. B. (1986). The three faces of thinking. *Journal of Higher Education*, *57*, 79-92.

Kruse, J., & Presseisen, B. Z. (1987). *A catalog of programs for teaching thinking.* Philadelphia, PA: Research for Better Schools.

Kuhn, D. (1978). Mechanisms of cognitive and social development: One psychology or two? *Human Development*, *21*, 92-118.

Kuhn, D. (1972). Mechanisms of change in the development of cognitive structures. *Child Development*, *43*, 833-844.

Larking, J. H. (1979). Information processing models and science instruction. In J. Lochhead & J. Clement (Eds.), *Cognitive process instruction: Research on teaching thinking skills*. Philadelphia, PA: Franklin Institute Press.

Lehman, D. R., Lempert, R. O., & Nisbett, R. E. (1988). The effects of graduate training on reasoning: Formal discipline and thinking about everyday life events. *American Psychologist*, *43*, 431-442.

Lipman, M., Sharp, A. M., & Oscanyan, F. (1980). *Philosophy in the classroom.* Philadelphia, PA: Temple University Press.

Lochhead, J., & Clement, J. (Eds.). (1979). *Cognitive process instruction: Research on teaching thinking skills.* Philadelphia, PA: Franklin Institute Press.

Marland, P. W., & Edwards, J. (1986). Students' in-class thinking. *Instructional Science*, 15, 75-88.

Mayer, R. E. (1988, August). *Teaching for thinking: Research on the teachability of thinking skills.* G. Stanley Hall Lecture presented at the annual meeting of the American Psychological Association, Atlanta, GA.

McMillan, J. H. (1987). Enhancing college students' critical thinking: A review of studies. *Research in Higher Education, 26,* 3-29.

McPeck, J. (1981). *Critical thinking and education.* Oxford, England: Martin Robinson.

Minstrell, J. (1982). Conceptual development research in the neutral setting of the classroom. In M. B. Rowe (Ed.). *Education in the '80s-science.* Washington, DC: National Education Association.

Modjeski, R. B., & Michael, W. B. (1983). An evaluation by a panel of psychologist of the reliability and validity of two tests of critical thinking. *Educational and Psychological Measurement, 43,* 1187-1197.

Morgenstern, C. F., & Renner, J. W. (1984). Measuring thinking with standardized science tests. *Journal of Research in Science Teaching, 21,* 639-648.

Newmann, F. M. (in press). Higher order thinking in the teaching of social studies: Connections between theory and practice. In J. Voss, D. Perkins, & J. Segal (Eds.), *Informal reasoning and education.* Hillsdale, NJ: Erlbaum.

Nisbett, R. E., & Wilson, T. D. (1977). Telling more than we can know: Verbal reports on mental processes. *Psychological Review, 84,* 231-259.

Nisbett, R. E., Fong, G. T., Lehman, D. R., & Cheng, P. W. (1987). Teaching reasoning. *Science, 238,* 625-631.

Nickerson, R. S., Perkins, D., & Smith, E. E. (1985). *The teaching of thinking.* Hillsdale, NJ: Erlbaum.

Norris, S. P. (in press). Informal reasoning assessment: Using verbal reports of thinking to improve multiple-choice test validity. In D. N. Perkins, J. Segal, & J. F. Voss (Eds.), *Informal reasoning and education.* Hillsdale, NJ: Erlbaum.

Norris, S. P. (1989). Can we test validly for critical thinking? *Educational Researcher, 18,* 21-26.

Norris, S. P. (1988). Controlling for background beliefs when developing multiple-choice critical thinking tests. *Educational Measurement Issues and Practice, 7,* 5-11.

Norris, S. P. (1988). Research needed on critical thinking. *Canadian Journal of Education, 13,* 125-137.

Norris, S. P., & Ennis, R. H. (in press). *Evaluating critical thinking.* Pacific Grove, CA: Midwest.

Norris, S. P., & Phillips, L. M. (1987). Explanations of reading comprehension: Schema theory and critical thinking theory. *Teachers College Record, 89,* 281-306.

Oliver, D. W., & Shaver, J. P. (1974). *Teaching public issues in the high school.* Boston, MA: Houghton Mifflin.

O'Reilly, K. (1985). *Critical thinking in American history.* Beverly, MA: Critical Thinking Press.

Paul, R. W. (1984). Critical thinking: Fundamental to education for a free society. *Educational Leadership. 42,* 4-14.

Paul, R. W. (1985). The critical thinking movement: A historical perspective. *National Forum, 65,* 2-3.

Perkins, D. N., & Salomon, G. (1989). Are cognitive skills context-bound? *Educational Researcher, 18,* 16-25.

Perkins, D. N., Allen, R., & Hafner, J. (1983). Difficulties in everyday reasoning. In W. Maxwell (Ed.), *Thinking: The expanding frontier.* Philadelphia, PA: Franklin Institute Press.

Perkins, D. N., Lochhead, J., & Bishop, J. C. (Eds.). (1987). *Thinking.* The second international conference. Hillsdale, NJ: Lawrence Erlbaum Associates.

Perry, W. G. (1981). *Cognitive and ethical growth: The making of meaning.* In A. W. Chickering, The Modern American College. San Francisco: Jossey-Bass.

Peterson, P. L., & Comeaux, M. A. (1987). Teachers' schemata for classroom events: The mental scaffolding of teachers' thinking during classroom instruction. Annual meeting of the American Educational Research Association: Teacher thinking; Relationships among schemata, routines, and teaching effectiveness. *Teaching and Teacher Education, 3,* 319-331.

Petrie, H. (1986). Testing for critical thinking. In D. Nyberg (Ed.), *Philosophy of Education* (1985), pp. 3-19. Normal, IL: Philosophy of Education Society.

Pierce, W., Lemke, E., & Smith, R. (1988). Critical thinking and moral development in secondary students. *High School Journal, 71*, 120-126.

Powell, S. (1987). Improving critical thinking: A review. *Educational Psychology, 7*, 169-185.

Pratt, M. W., Golding, G., Hunter, W., & Norris, J. (1988). From inquiry to judgment: Age and sex differences in patterns of adult moral thinking and information seeking. *International Journal of Aging and Human Development, 27*, 108-124.

Presseisen, B. Z. (1986). *Critical thinking and thinking skills: State of the art definitions and practice in public schools*. Philadelphia, PA: Research for Better Schools.

Presseisen, B. Z. (1987). *Thinking skills throughout the curriculum. A conceptual design*. Bloomington, IN: Pi Lambda Theta.

Raths, L. E., Wasserman, S., Jonas, A., & Rothstein, A. (1986). *Teaching for thinking* (2nd ed.). New York: Teachers College, Columbia University.

Read, S. J. (1987). Constructing causal scenarios: A knowledge structure approach to causal reasoning. *Journal of Personality, 52*, 288-302.

Resnick, L. B. (1987). Constructing knowledge in school. In L. S. Liben (Ed.), *Development and learning: Conflict or congruence*? Hillsdale, NJ: Erlbaum.

Resnick, L. B. (1987). *Education and learning to think*. Washington, DC: National Academy Press.

Rokeach, M. (1960). *The open and closed mind*. New York: Basic Books.

Roth, K. J. (1986). *Conceptual-change learning and student processing of science texts* (Research Series No. 167). East Lansing, MI: The Institute for Research on Thinking.

Ruggiero, V. R. (1984). *The art of thinking: A guide to critical and creative thought*. New York: Harper & Row.

Runco, M. A., & Okuda, S. M. (1988). Problem discovery, divergent thinking, and the creative process. *Journal of Youth and Adolescence, 17*, 211-220.

Scholnick, E. K. (1987). The language of mind: Statements about mental states. Special Issue: The language of thinking: Mental state words. *Discourse Processes, 10*, 181-192.

Schrag, F. (1989). Are there levels of thinking? *Teachers College Record, 90*, 529-533.

Schrag, F. (1988). *Thinking in School and Society.* New York: Routlege.

Segal, J. W., Chipman, S. F., & Glaser, R. (Eds.). (1985). *Thinking and learning skills: Vol. I. Relating instruction to research.* Hillsdale, NJ: Erlbaum.

Shawyer, G., Booth, M., Brown, R. (1988). The development of children's historical thinking. *Cambridge Journal of Education, 18*, 209-219.

Siegel, H. (1980, November). Critical thinking as educational ideal. *The Educational Forum*, pp. 7-23.

Sternberg, R. J., & Bhana, K. (1986). Synthesis of research on the effectiveness of intellectual skills programs: Snake-oil remedies or miracle cures? *Educational Leadership, 44*, 60-67.

Sternberg, R. J., & Smith, E. E. (Eds.). (1988). *The psychology of human thought.* New York: Cambridge University Press.

Sternberg, R. J., & Wagner, R. K. (Eds.). (1986). *Practical intelligence: Nature and origins of competence in the everyday world.* New York: Cambridge University Press.

Svensson, L. (1985). The role of experience in adult thinking about evidence for causal interpretations. *Human Learning Journal of Practical Research and Applications, 4*, 187-201.

Tennyson, R. O., Thurlow, R., & Breuer, K. (1987). Problem-oriented simulations to develop and improve higher-order thinking strategies. *Computers in Human Behavior*, 3, 151-165.

Tierney, R. J., Soter, A., O'Flahavan, J. F., McGinley, W. (1989). The effects of reading and writing upon thinking critically. *Reading Research Quarterly, 24*, 134-173.

Trabasso, T., & Van den Broek, P. (1985). Causal thinking and the representation of narrative events. *Journal of Memory and Language*, *24*, 612-630.

# INDEX